D1355608

THE TRUTH ABOUT
GETTING THINGS DONE

Mark Fritz

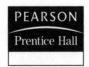

PEARSON
Prentice Hall

Harlow, England • London • New York • Boston • San Francisco • Toronto
Sydney • Tokyo • Singapore • Hong Kong • Seoul • Taipei • New Delhi
Cape Town • Madrid • Mexico City • Amsterdam • Munich • Paris • Milan

PEARSON EDUCATION LIMITED

Edinburgh Gate
Harlow CM20 2JE
Tel: +44 (0)1279 623623
Fax: +44 (0)1279 431059
Website: www.pearsoned.co.uk

First published in Great Britain in 2008

© Procedor Limited 2008

The right of Mark Fritz to be identifed as author of this work has been asserted by him in accordance with the Copyright, Designs and Patents Act 1988.

ISBN: 978-0-273-71839-0

British Library Cataloguing-in-Publication Data
A catalogue record for this book is available from the British Library

Library of Congress Cataloging-in-Publication Data
Fritz, Mark.
  The truth about getting things done / Mark Fritz.
    p. cm.
  Includes bibliographical references
  ISBN 978-0-273-71839-0 (pbk. : alk. paper) 1. Motivation (Psychology) 2. Self-actualization (Psychology) 3. Self-management (Psychology) 4. Life skills. I. Title.
  BF503.F757 2008
  153.8--dc22   2008026844

10 9 8 7 6 5 4 3 2 1
12 11 10 09 08

Typeset in 10/13 pt Meta-LightLF by 3
Printed and bound in Great Britain by Ashford Colour Press Ltd, Gosport, Hants

The publisher's policy is to use paper manufactured from sustainable forests.

To a very inspirational leader . . .

Peter Meier

. . . Someone who understands and lives the Truths of Getting Things Done and inspires the belief in others that anything is possible.

"I just don't have the time!" A very common phrase that you probably say quite often and hear others say as well. The fast pace of life today and everyone wanting to do the most they can, means that you don't always get done what you would have liked to get done. However, some people seem to get more done than others, and you never hear them say, "I just don't have the time!" To them, it is never a time problem, but what the time is used for. How about you?

Time management is just a myth. Everyone gets the same amount of time each day, and nobody can really manage time. You cannot take 30 hours today because you are really busy, and then take only 18 hours on Friday, because you are going to have an easy day. It just doesn't work that way. So, you can't manage time, but you can manage how you use it.

Is your goal just to get more things done? For some, that seems to be their aim. For the successful people in the world, it is not the complete story. For the successful people, the goal is not just getting things done, but getting the *right* things done.

This book is all about getting the *right* things done.

I've studied how the most successful people get things done, as well as the time management gurus who have all those techniques to, as they say, *manage your time better*. I have tried and thrown away many of those time management techniques, and realised that the way to get things done is never about how many of the techniques you know; it is about keeping a focus on what is the most important to get done.

This book will convince you, as I have been convinced, that you *cannot* really manage your time, but you *can* manage the focus of how you use your time. You will see that getting things done comes down to five key factors, which you will understand in much greater detail as you read through the book:

1. **Success**—Knowing what you want provides the reason behind what you want to get done.

2. **Thought**—All action begins in our thoughts first, so thinking is a great way to use your time.

3. **Discipline**—You get things done by disciplining yourself to do what you know you should do.

4. **Teamwork**—No one achieves success and gets the *right* things done without the help of others.

5. **Growth**—The more you grow, the more experience you gain to focus on the *right* things.

As you read this book, you too will be convinced that getting things done does not begin with time management, but with *focus* management, and then having the *discipline* to do what is necessary, when it is necessary. You will no longer tell yourself, "I just don't have the time!" Instead, you will start, from the very day you finish the book, to invest time in determining your focus and then reminding yourself of that focus each and every day. Just as other successful people have done, you can too.

Here's to you—to getting the *right* things done.

TRUTH

1

It's not about getting things done, it's about success

Life is not about activity, but about *accomplishment* and getting the *right* things done. In order to create the life you want, everything starts by defining what *success* really means to you. Defining what success means to you can provide you with a focus on how to create the life you would like to live and what you would like to achieve (getting the *right* things done).

There are many people who go through life not really knowing what they want. In fact, most people would have some difficulty in telling you specifically what they want in life. However, these same people could probably make a very long list of what they don't want. Think about this? If you can make a very long list of what you don't want, then you would have to admit that you probably do more thinking about what you don't want than what you really do want. Does this sound like you?

To be truly successful and to make sure you are getting the right things done, it is important to invest the time in thinking through exactly what success means to you. Defining what success means to you can help bring your life more meaning and help you channel all your energy into getting the *right* things done. Remember, you can never live your life to its fullest by living according to someone else's definition of success, not your parent's, not your friend's. It is all about what you want, and everything starts with *you defining success for you.*

When you look at defining success, you always need to look at it from a balanced point of view. There are a great number of people who have achieved very big professional and financial success, only to wish later in life that they had made more time to spend with their family and friends. Take a look at both parts of your life, both the personal and the professional, and think about what a successful life would look like and what you would like to achieve.

> Think about what a successful life would look like and what you would like to achieve.

There are two key factors in defining success for you: your **passion** and your **potential**.

If you were to ask very successful people what was one of the keys to their success, many of them might say the following: "I made a career (or created a business) around my passion." Those who have built their life around their **passion** always get more accomplished and achieve greater success than those who don't.

You can probably see the power behind building a life around your passion, by taking your own life as an example. Don't you feel more inspired and get more energy from doing the things that you are passionate about? Wouldn't you procrastinate less and be much better at getting things done if you were spending more of your time on what you are passionate about than on what you are not? You can see the power behind creating a life around your passion.

The second key factor is your **potential**. Too many people define success based on what they have today and what they might be able to do. The truly successful people always define success based on the full potential that is inside them. Speaker and author Nido Qubein said it best: "The trouble with many plans is that they are based on the way things are now. To be successful, your personal plan must focus on what you want, not what you have." Like so many others, you have great potential inside you to do many things that you would have never thought possible.

Remember, you can never truly reach something that is never defined. The place to start is to invest time in some quality thinking around your passion and your potential, as well as defining what things are most

> You can never truly reach something that is never defined.

important to you for your life. You are defining success in terms of what you would like to achieve in your life and then also designing the life that will make it happen. A great place to start is always just to do a little brainstorming on the following and to write your ideas down on paper:

1. What does the word success mean to me?
2. What am I really passionate about?

3. What gives me energy when I am doing it instead of taking my energy?

4. What have I always dreamed about accomplishing, but haven't really thought about how to do?

5. What potential do I see inside me and what have others told me about my potential in the past?

The clear *what* (success) provides meaning to get the *right* things done.

If you have not done so already, invest the time to:

1. Define your passion and what's most important to you.

2. Think in terms of your full potential, and not just where you are today.

3. Define success and design your life, in terms of both what you want to achieve and how to get it.

TRUTH

2

The why needs to be
greater than the how

There are far too many people who go through life just *going through the motions*. They have developed their daily habits over time, and their habits have become their life. These people have never really taken the time to think about *what* they want and *why* they want it. How about you?

For you to accomplish what you want in life, the *why* is more important than the *how*. In fact, to achieve the success you want, the *why* always needs to be greater than the *how*.

The *why* is a powerful motivator and is the biggest factor to getting the *right* things done. Take an example of a person who contracted lung cancer from smoking for many years. The very day this person received the news about the cancer, he or she just quit smoking, right then. Why? The news of the cancer, and the fact that smoking became a life or death issue, made the *why* finally big enough to stop smoking, and stop right away. You can see the power behind a big *why*.

However, you don't always have a life or death situation, but you do have some very important things in your life that you want to accomplish. Very often you have dreamed about achieving something, and have even pictured the end result in your mind. If you have kept it only as a dream and have not invested any thinking time on the *why*, you probably haven't taken very much action towards that dream. Also, to achieve that dream, you will most likely need to change what you are currently doing today with your time, and you may even need to create some new habits.

To make the necessary changes or to create the new habits to achieve your dream, you need to build the *why* big enough in order to take the necessary actions to achieve it. The *why* needs to be big and strong enough for you to change your behaviours and to repeat those behaviours frequently and long enough to put the new necessary habits into your daily life. The example of the *why*, for the person with cancer, shows that a *why* can be powerful enough to change behaviour right away.

> For you to accomplish what you want in life, the *why* is more important than the *how*.

The *why* is not only important in driving the actions needed to achieve what you want, it can also be a powerful driver of the creativity in you. The bigger the *why* you have behind what you want, the more you make this a focus for you, and the more thinking you will do on it. The more time thinking on what you want will always help you to see new and better ways to achieve it.

That's the power behind building the *why*. A big and strong *why* creates the need so powerful in your mind (both the conscious and subconscious mind) that you have to have it and you will do any *how* in order to get it. When you have to have it, you begin to take the necessary actions to get it, and you also begin not to let other feelings stop you. The *why* has then become so strong that you will do even the things you hate in order to get what you want.

The *why* powers the *what* and gives you energy to do the *how*. The Friedrich Nietzche quote says it all: "He who has the why to live can bear with almost any how." You see this in many of the most successful athletes.

> The *why* powers the *what* and gives you energy to do the *how*.

They will say that they often hate the training they have to do, but they love even more the feeling of winning and being number one. Their *why* of winning and being number one is more powerful than the feelings they get while doing the training they hate.

For your dreams or for whatever else you want to accomplish in your life, the first step is always to build the *why* before starting on the *how*. A big and powerful *why* provides you with the motivation to take the necessary and repeated actions, and to do whatever it takes to achieve what you want.

For whatever you want to accomplish in your life:

1. Start by building your *why* today.
2. The *why* provides you with the drive to do the *how*.
3. The *why* always needs to be greater than the *how*.

TRUTH

3

You need to believe it in
order to achieve it

There's a very common saying that all of us have said at least once, "I will believe it when I see it." However, success in life works in exactly the opposite way. You need to believe that you can have the life you want and accomplish what you want before you will see how to achieve it. The most powerful saying is then, "I will see it when I believe it."

An old story that highlights this very well is about the two shoe sales people who went to a remote part of Africa. One writes back to headquarters, no one wears shoes here, there's no market. The other one writes back, no one wears shoes here, there's a fantastic market opportunity. Please send me more samples. You can see that the second sales person had a totally different belief and saw something the other sales person didn't.

How about you and what you want in your life, and what you want to accomplish? If you don't believe you can accomplish what you want and live the life you want, do you think you will see the things that will help you get it?

You can see examples of why it is so important to believe it in the sports world. All of today's best athletes are using visualisation techniques to picture running that perfect race, or kicking that game-winning goal into the net. Every time they are visualising the success in their mind, they are really creating another layer of the belief in their mind that they can do it. The belief that propels them to success in their sport didn't come to them in a flash. It was the constant repeating of that winning visualisation that created a belief strong enough in them in order to carry it out in reality.

You can do the same for yourself. Why not invest time each day and visualise the achievement and the living of the success you want for your life? By doing the same constant repeating of this success visualisation, you will build the belief inside you just as powerful as the successful athletes do.

When you believe it, you then see how you can achieve it, and begin taking the actions to get it done.

> When you believe it, you then see how you can achieve it, and begin taking the actions to get it done.

Belief is so very powerful and something that engages not only your conscious mind, but your subconscious mind as well. Let's say that you have defined success for yourself, defined the *why* behind it, and have been creating the layers of belief inside you that you can achieve it. What you have done is created such a clear and powerful target in your mind that your subconscious can work on as well.

Your subconscious mind is really childlike. It only works on what you give it to work on. If you give it a very clear and powerful target, it has something clear and powerful to work on.

Let's take the example of when you bought your last car. You studied the brochure, took the test drive and fell in love with the idea (the picture) of owning that car. You were building *why* you needed to buy that car.

By the time you bought the car, the *why* was so big that you would have felt terrible if you didn't buy it. You probably started to notice, as you were driving around at that time, many more cars like the one you had just bought. Interesting, but the same number of that type of car were on the road just months before, but you never noticed them. Why? Because you built the *why* so strong on needing that car that your subconscious mind was pointing them out to you everywhere you drove. You didn't get up in the morning and decide to go and look for that type of car all day long, did you? Your subconscious mind pointed them out without you even thinking of it.

The same thing happens when you have such a strong belief. Your strong belief becomes such a powerful focus for your subconscious mind to act upon. As you go through your day, your subconscious mind is pointing out people you meet and situations that can help you reach what you want. If you believe strongly enough, your subconscious mind will help you see it and achieve it.

> If you believe strongly enough, your subconscious mind will help you see it and achieve it.

You can imagine the power behind building the belief to achieve what you want. The more time you invest in building the belief in getting what you want, the more opportunities you will see to achieve it.

Remember, you can never really see what will create the success for you if you do not have the belief inside you first. Believe it in order to see it.

Success doesn't require proof, just belief. Build the belief by:

1. Focusing your mind every day on what you want.
2. Repeating to yourself why you want it and why it is important to you.
3. Picturing your life as if you already have what you want—visualise it.

TRUTH

4

It's focus management, not time management

No one can manage time. You can't say to yourself that you will be really busy today, and take 30 hours for today; and that tomorrow doesn't look too bad, so 18 hours will do. You cannot manage time. However, you can manage your focus, and your focus determines how you will use your time.

While everyone gets the same amount of time, there are those people who get much more accomplished using it than others. Why is that? Time is almost always not the problem in getting things done. It is how you use your time that is.

> Time is almost always not the problem in getting things done. It is how you use your time that is.

There are so many time management ideas, techniques and software you can use to help you manage your time better. For those who know of the 80/20 rule, 80 per cent of the power behind your getting things done is not about using any of those time management ideas, techniques or software. What it is about is creating and maintaining your focus on what's most important to you and what will move you closer to the success you want to achieve and the life you want to live. It is really about what you decide to use your time for.

How you use your time is based on the choices you make on a daily, hourly and minute by minute basis, on what you choose to do and what you choose not to do. How you determine what you say "yes" to do and what you say "no" to do is what really determines what you can and will accomplish. What you determine as your focus can be a powerful criterion from which you can base what you say yes and no to. Without a focus, you don't have any criteria as to what should and shouldn't get done.

What really is your focus? Your main focus (or criterion) is based on the success you desire, in terms of both what you want to achieve and the lifestyle you would like to live. This focus helps you determine what you say yes and no to. To achieve the success you have defined, you want to focus your time on doing more activities that take you closer to it. Most people don't accomplish what they want because they lack this focus. People without a clear focus will often say yes to things that really aren't getting them closer to what they want, and then are always amazed at the end of each day, as they didn't get to do anything that they really wanted to do. They were actually working to other people's focus and not their own.

Also, remember that your focus is based on what you want (both professionally and personally). You want to make sure that you have the right balance on that focus, to ensure you keep the right perspective for the work/life balance that works best for you.

There are many ways to capture your focus so that it can be a constant reminder on how best to use your time. Some people have Post-it note reminders, others always keep a list in front of them, and yet there are many people who always want to keep it just in their head. The key is to find the best way that works for you, and experience has shown that getting it out of your head and down on paper somewhere is often one of the best ways.

If you are like most others, you will make the right choices on how to use your time when you have that clear focus. Find the way to remind yourself of your focus and then make it a habit. More than any other thing you could do, creating and maintaining your focus will enable you to get more done, and the *right* things done.

Your focus becomes the criterion you use as a daily basis for what you say yes or no to. A clear "laser" focus enables you to achieve more of what you want to achieve.

A clear "laser" focus enables you to achieve more of what you want to achieve.

Remember, it is not possible to manage time. However, you can manage your focus by:

1. Determining your focus based on the success you desire.
2. Remembering that your focus is always a balance of both your professional and personal lives.
3. Using your focus as your *criterion* for saying either yes or no.

TRUTH

5

If everything is important,
then nothing is important

If everything is important, then everything is at the same level. If everything is at the same level, then there is nothing that is really different—or important. The most important thing for you to do is have a good way of defining what's most important to you. To get the *right* things done, you need to understand what the most important things are that need to get done, and do those things first—the *right* things.

> The most important thing for you to do is have a good way of defining what's most important to you.

There's an old story that has been told in many different ways. Here's a version that highlights the power behind a focus and understanding what's important.

A professor brings a large glass jar into class and puts it on the table in front of him. He fills the jar all the way to the top with big rocks, and asks the class, "Is the jar full?" The class says, "Yes, it looks full to us." Then, the professor pours small pebbles into the jar. The small pebbles fill in between the big rocks all around in the jar, and the professor fills the small pebbles all the way to the top of the jar. Again he asks, "Is the jar full?" This time the class doesn't answer, as they are not sure any more.

Next, the professor fills the jar with sand. The sand fills in all around the rocks and pebbles, and the professor fills the jar with sand all the way to the top. The professor asks, "Is the jar *now* full?" The class is silent. Finally, the professor begins to pour water into the jar. The water soaks the sand and he continues to pour water into the jar until the jar is full. Again the professor asks, "Is the jar full?"

In conclusion, he asks the class why he showed this example, and one of the students makes a joke and says, "To show how much you can fit in a jar." The professor says, "That's true, but it also represents what you can fit in your life, when you get the rocks in first."

The rocks represent what is *important* in your life and the fact that they need to go into your life first. Taking the example of the jar, would it have been possible for all the big rocks to fit into the jar if they were put in last, not first (if the sand and water were filled first)?

Probably not, and the same is true for your life. If you fill your day with all the things that aren't important (maybe other people's rocks), there will be no room for what is most important to you.

Most people do not invest the time to really determine what is most important to them. If you never determine what is important, then everything looks at the same level of importance to you. When everything looks the same, the urgent always seems to get done first. In your own life, if you only did the urgent each and every day, is it going to take you to what you want, that success, and fast enough?

Let's take an example that highlights the power behind doing what's important first.

You have had a very busy day, but you've been working on what you consider as sand and water, other people's rocks, and are feeling a little frustrated. Your partner or friend calls up and asks you to do a couple of errands on the way home from work (pick up the dry cleaning, get something for dinner, etc.). You have more of what you consider sand and water piled on to your day, and this is frustrating you even more.

Consider a different day. You have been working on the big rocks from the beginning of the day, fitting in all the pebbles, sand and water around the rocks. You have the feeling of getting things done, the *right* things. Your partner or friend calls up and asks the very same things, as mentioned above, but this time it doesn't frustrate you. Why? Because you put the most important tasks first into your day and you have the feeling of getting done what *you* wanted to get done.

Life is not about just getting things done; it is about getting the *right* things done. Everything you can do to keep the most important tasks in front of you will help you do the most important first. Whenever the important tasks are not in your focus, then the urgent and easy to do always seem to get done first. The real key is always to bring the important to the same level as the urgent and easy to do.

Find the way that works best for you, by constantly reviewing your focus for what's important and always reminding yourself of that focus. The more the important is in your focus, the more you will do the important.

Don't be driven by the urgent and by what other people think is important. Bring your important to the same level as the urgent.

Put the reminder habits in your life, to make sure you always remember what is important, by:

> The more the important is in your focus, the more you will do the important.

1. Keep reminding yourself what's important.

2. Remembering that getting the *right* things done is often about what you say "no" to.

3. Realising that if everything is important, then really nothing is important.

TRUTH

6

Your clarity of focus drives the action you want

Your focus is what helps you to determine the important from the unimportant. When that focus is crystal clear, it also drives you to take more action on the important, and this helps you to get more done of what you want to get done. With your busy life these days, and with everything that hits you from both a professional and personal perspective, it can be easy for you to lose track of your focus.

Clarity is the key word here because without it, you will never achieve as much as you can. You can see examples of both good and poor clarity in all parts of your life.

Clarity is the key word here because without it, you will never achieve as much as you can.

If you have children and are explaining something to them, the clearer you are the more likely they will follow what you say, and do what you want them to do. How many times have you been in a hurry, haven't taken the time to explain something clearly, and then your children haven't followed through and done what you said? It wasn't really clear for them and if you had had the time to think about it yourself, it probably wouldn't have been clear to you either.

You also see this in the business world every day at the end of meetings. The time has run out, and there is such a rush to conclude the meeting quickly and move on to the next one. Someone wraps up with some vague directions on what needs to be done and everyone looks at each other as if to ask, "Who really has the action?" Another example of things not being clear.

These examples highlight the need for clarity in order to be good at getting things done, and clarity always begins with your focus. This is really the criterion by which you say either "yes" or "no" to everything that hits you each day. The clearer your focus, the better decisions you will make on what you say yes to and what you say no to, and this results in your doing more of what's important to you. When your focus is not as clear, you have a very fuzzy criterion to use in making those yes/no decisions. Then, you will likely be saying yes to many things that are not really that important for you to do.

If the clarity of your focus is this important, you should put ways into your daily and weekly life to create that clarity and maintain it.

Clarity always helps you to bring to use the power of your subconscious mind as well. The subconscious mind can help you, but only if it gets something clear to work on. The clearer your focus, the more help you get from your subconscious mind to develop those creative ideas to get more things done. This is why when you go to bed with a very clear problem that needs to be solved, you often wake up with the answer. Why? Because you gave your subconscious mind something very clear to work on.

Also, the clarity in your focus should always be covering both the *what* and the *why*. The *what* are the focus areas that will drive you to complete all the things you need to get done. However, by also focusing on the *why*, you create even more inspiration and energy behind the work needed to complete the tasks. It is always a great idea to cover both the *what* and *why* for the big things you need to accomplish in your life. They bring both clarity and inspiration to *get it done*.

> The clarity in your focus should always be covering both the *what* and the *why*.

Another key benefit of having the right clarity of focus is the clarity it brings to the trade-offs you need to make in how you use your time. Saying yes to something also means saying no to something else. When you constantly keep a clear focus, you will understand much better the trade-offs you are making based on your yes/no decisions. If you feel better about those yes/no decisions you will have less stress, since if something is not getting done, you know this is because it isn't as high a priority for you based on your focus.

Remember, the clarity of your focus drives you to take more action on what you want than on what others want. Clarity drives achievement. No one accomplishes a vague goal.

Invest the time to make the *what* and *why* clear for you.

1. Continually review your focus for clarity.
2. Always cover both the *what* and the *why*.
3. Remember that a clear focus drives clear action.

TRUTH

7

Goals make your life
self-directed

Having a clear focus is important. However, what really gives power to that focus are the goals you create based on your focus. Goals help you keep the direction of your life in line with your focus, and also create a sense of urgency that drives your daily and weekly actions. Goals put you in the driver's seat of your life. Without them, you are in the passenger seat, the back seat, or maybe not even in the car.

> Goals put you in the driver's seat of your life.

There's a great way to look at the criteria for the big goals in your life.

Your goals should *excite* you and *scare* you at the same time.

You will never do something well or have the energy to keep at it, unless it gets you excited. Look at defining goals that really *excite* you and these are usually around those things that you are passionate about.

Your goals should also *scare* you at the same time. Goals should challenge you to grow, and if you already know specifically how to achieve something, it is really not a goal. It is then simply an outcome that you have the plan to achieve.

A goal is something that should challenge you to grow and use the potential that is inside you. At the time you create the goal, you probably don't really know exactly how you will reach it. When US President John F. Kennedy made the speech in 1961 about America putting a man on the moon by the end of the decade, that was a goal. Do you think President Kennedy and NASA knew exactly how to do it right then? Probably not, and for your goals, you probably won't know either. That's the scary part.

What you have also learned about President Kennedy's goal is that he created a time limit on it. Attaching a date to your big goals will create a sense of urgency that puts the power and drive behind your daily and weekly actions.

You want to make sure you have a third criterion for each of your goals, a *By When*.

Remember, make sure that your big goals both excite you and scare you, and when you build your life around those goals, you make your life self-directed. These big goals will keep you focused on what you want to achieve and help create the direction your life will take.

> **Make sure that your big goals both excite you and scare you.**

In response to President Kennedy's goal, NASA needed to define some smaller intermediate goals in order to make sure they could both meet the end of the decade timeline and motivate their people to achieve it. NASA defined some key intermediate goals, and you will need to do the same for your big goals as well.

There are a few other attributes of goals that help drive you to achieve them. They are:

1. **Clarity**—Your goals need to be clear, as you cannot reach a vague goal or get motivated by it. Also, you need to define it in such a way that it is clear to you when it is achieved. The key here is that if you can't measure its achievement, then the goal is not defined clearly enough.

2. **Review**—Goals are not something that are set and then not looked at again for a year. In order to keep your life self-directed, goals are something that you need to review often, and for some daily. Goals need to be reviewed often, as this is another way to remind yourself of your focus and what is most important to you. As best-selling author and international speaker Brian Tracy says, "The very act of setting goals and writing them down increases your likelihood of achieving them by about 10 times."

Written goals and plans are very powerful, as they set both direction and pace, as well as put you into the driver's seat of your life.

Goals are like the *roadmap for your life*. Write down:

1. Big goals that both excite and scare you.

2. Those intermediate goals that will help you make progress and motivate you to achieve them.

3. How and when you will review them. (Why not daily?)

TRUTH

8

Life is about the journey and the destination

There are successful people who had only the destination in their minds. They worked very hard, made a great deal of money, and then woke up one day only to ask themselves, "Was it worth it?" They were singularly focused on what they wanted to achieve (the destination) and forgot that life is also about the journey.

Happiness and fulfilment cannot only be yours when you achieve success or reach your goals; it has to be there during the journey as well. Truly happy people have learned to enjoy the journey and the destination, as life is really about both.

> Truly happy people have learned to enjoy the journey and the destination, as life is really about both.

Earl Nightingale, who recorded 'The Strangest Secret', put it best when he said, "Success is the progressive realization of a worthy goal or ideal." It is never only about the destination, and a successful life is always defined in terms of both the journey and the destination. If you were to think that you could only be happy when you achieve your goal or reach the success you desire, then you would only really be happy for a very short time. You would be happy only at the moment you achieved it.

You could say that it is all about designing the life that you would like to live. What would your life look like if you could design it? This is a great question, and if you are like most people, you haven't invested that much time in answering it. So, why not answer it *now*?

You know that it is important to have that target in your mind of what you want to accomplish and what success in your life would look like for you. You also know that understanding your passion and potential are important in defining success for your life. To move forward in designing your life, you want to think about two very important things. They are:

1. **What makes you happy?**—What relationships, what activities, etc. provide you with the most enjoyment?

2. **What helps you to grow?**—What personal development or activities will help you grow (and faster)?

In creating that life you want, it is all about putting into your daily activities more of what makes you happy and helps you grow.

Remember, you are really designing a life that both reaches the destination and enjoys the trip. Invest the time to design your life upfront and you will always be enjoying the journey. Jim Rohn, America's foremost business philosopher, said it best: "Learn how to be happy with what you have while you pursue all that you want."

> Life is about reaching your potential and enjoying the trip.

Life is about reaching your potential and enjoying the trip. Make sure you have an enjoyable and rewarding journey by:

1. Aligning your life behind your passions and potential.

2. Including in your life those activities that make you *happy*.

3. Including in your life those activities that help you *grow*.

9

You accomplish more with
an outcome focus

Have you noticed people who seem to be busy all the time, but you wonder what they are really accomplishing, the outcomes? There's a huge difference between having an activity or an outcome approach to your day and your life. Those people who choose to have an outcome focus get more done because they are more focused on what they are busy for.

The more you take an outcome focus, the clearer the target you have, and the more ownership you will take for it getting accomplished as well. Outcomes drive ownership, and ownership drives results.

Outcomes drive ownership, and ownership drives results.

So, why do people continue to take an activity focus when they know that they could get more done with an outcome focus? Because, as Henry Ford said, "Thinking is the hardest work there is, which is the probable reason so few engage in it." It is because defining outcomes and using them to drive what you do, means that you have to invest some quality time to think about the key outcomes that are most important to you.

Most people don't invest the time to *think*! Sounds strange, but with the fast pace of life, many people are focused just on doing activities and don't really take the time to think. Also, if you are not thinking, you are constantly doing things out of habit (the same things) and you will always get the same results, unless you change your habits.

The most successful people are the ones who get the most accomplished, and they view their thinking time for deciding the key outcomes they want to accomplish as one of the most important things to put first into their day and week. How about you?

The more clearly you define your outcomes, the more creativity you will drive within you to achieve them, as it is difficult to get really creative around a vague target. Therefore, to get more creative and find better and faster ways to achieve your key outcomes, you have to define your outcomes as clearly as you possibly can.

When you have clear outcomes, you will be getting lots of ideas on how to achieve them. The key then is to get them out of your head and down on paper somewhere. If you just keep them in your head, you might forget them, and especially at the very time when you could have used the idea to take the *right* action and get it done.

Very often a picture of the outcome you are trying to achieve will drive even more creativity. This is why you see many people with pictures of the car they want to buy, or the home they want to purchase. With a picture, you drive both your creativity and the motivation inside you to take action and go get it.

> **The more clearly you define your outcomes, the more creativity you will drive within you to achieve them.**

Decide today when and how you will invest time to think about the key outcomes to accomplish that will take you closer to the success and goals that you have defined. The clearer the outcomes you define, the more creativity you will trigger within you, and the more ideas you will get to take action on. Remember, only action is what gets things done, and by defining clear outcomes, you get more of the *right* things done.

It's all about accomplishment, not just completing activities. Remember:

1. For everything, take an outcome focus.
2. Outcomes drive ownership for accomplishment and results.
3. Always keep an outcome focus rather than an activity focus.

TRUTH

10

Nothing is stopping you but you

The biggest barrier to achieving the success you have defined for your life is never anyone else or the circumstances you encounter. Your biggest barrier is almost always *you*. Your belief in yourself is the only thing that can really stop you from achieving the success you want in your life and getting the *right* things done to achieve it. Dr Maxwell Maltz, author of *Psycho-Cybernetics*, put it best when he said, "Within you right now is the power to do things you never dreamed possible. This power becomes available to you just as soon as you can change your beliefs."

Everything you accomplish starts in your thoughts first. However, what drives your thoughts are your beliefs about what you think you can do and how you think you should act. These beliefs have been created over time, with many of them originating when you were very young and growing up to become an adult. When you were a child, you can remember that you thought almost anything was possible. As an adult, you seem to have narrowed greatly what you think is possible, and this can be a big factor in limiting what you can accomplish as well.

Robert H. Schuller, author of more than 30 books, said, "The only place where your dream becomes impossible is in your own thinking." What beliefs do you think are stopping you today? What would you do differently if those beliefs were not there or changed to something much more positive about what you could accomplish?

If you thought of the beliefs that are stopping you, the next step is to ask yourself *why*? You really cannot change your beliefs until you invest the time to think *why* you think that way. The *why* will uncover where these beliefs really started for you, and then you can see whether there is a strong basis for this belief, or whether it grew from something small into what it is today, just by repeating it.

> You really cannot change your beliefs until you invest the time to think *why* you think that way.

One of the biggest problems with the beliefs you have about yourself is that you have the natural tendency always to search out evidence of your beliefs in your daily life. If you have a belief that you cannot do something, then your mind will always be avoiding the situation where you might actually have to do that in your daily life. So, the more you are constantly telling yourself that you cannot do certain things, the more you are avoiding those very things in your daily life.

In fact, these are probably the very things that will take you closer to the success you desire and the goals you have defined, but because your beliefs are telling you that you cannot do them, you are avoiding having to do those things each and every day.

What's really happening is that your beliefs are narrowing down the possible actions you can take to achieve the success you want. The more limiting beliefs you have, the more you are limiting the actions you will take to get what you really want.

> The more limiting beliefs you have, the more you are limiting the actions you will take to get what you really want.

Les Brown, international motivational speaker and author, says, "Sometimes you've got to believe in someone else's belief in you until your own belief kicks in." Very often you just don't believe you can do it, but others around you have the belief in you that you can. It is important just to put your faith in others' belief in you and begin taking *action*, and then the action will help develop the belief in you to keep carrying it on.

Also, there's a great way to drive you into a new belief. It's called *as if*. Why not just think *as if* you are the person who already has achieved what you originally thought was not possible. When you believe *as if* you are the person already, you will begin both to think and to take the actions as that person would.

If you were to think *as if* you were already the person you would like to be, what would you be thinking about today and what are the actions you would be taking? Whatever you are thinking and whatever actions you think of, write them down *now*. This very action of thinking *as if* is getting you thinking and acting differently than you were just five minutes ago.

To create a different life, you need to begin with your beliefs. Remember, your beliefs drive your thinking, and your thinking drives your actions. Only you can really stop you.

Invest time to think through the *why* behind your limiting beliefs.

1. Think through what's stopping you from taking action right now.

2. Think *as if* and suddenly you will begin taking action *as if.*

3. Only *you* can ever stop *you.*

TRUTH

11

Your past does not have to equal your future

Many of your beliefs about what you can become or what you can accomplish are based on your past experiences. You probably hit the replay button on your life and often bring up those past bad experiences to remind yourself of what you think you cannot do. Remember, your past does not equal your future, and you and everyone else can only accomplish in the present (today).

You read stories all the time of people who changed their lives around and accomplished great success. They all had a past and if that had continued the same way, they would have never achieved what they did. However, they believed, and you can too, that their past did not have to equal their future.

Your past is only something that you can learn from. However, if you are like many others, you seem to replay your bad past experiences over and over again. You cannot really do any good in replaying past bad experiences, but somehow you keep doing it.

> Your past is only something that you can learn from.

When you learn something from the past, you have something you can use in the future to do things differently and hopefully better. In this way, your past can be very valuable for you in getting things done, but only if you learn from it, and think about how you can apply what you learned to future actions.

Here's the key: whenever you find yourself replaying a past experience, either bad or even good, why not ask yourself the question: "What did I learn from this experience and how can I use it in the future?" This makes your past experiences useful, and you can apply what you learned to do things better in the future.

Also, you will find that when you take what you learned from your past experiences, you will then start to do less replaying of those experiences. Your mind won't see the benefit as much any more, and the same drive to replay them will no longer be there either. Why? Because you learned something from the experience.

There's a great NLP (neuro-linguistic programming) technique that can help you learn from past events, and particularly those that were bad experiences for you. To describe it quickly here, you want to replay that particular event in your mind again. However, this time you want to look at it as if you were watching what happened in a movie theatre and someone else is playing the part of you. This helps you to take an objective view of what happened, and also helps you to see more easily what you can learn in that particular event, as you are then mentally not in the middle of it, but watching it happen.

This technique sounds a little strange, and you are probably saying to yourself—could it really work? It does, and when you watch the event as if you were in a movie theatre, the impact of that event on you becomes less as well. Why? Because you are making it less personal and looking at it as if it were someone else. That view of it being someone else helps you to learn from the experience faster.

Once you learn from your past bad experiences, forget them and focus on the present (today).

Remember, you can only accomplish something in the present. The past is only useful for what we learn from it on how to do a better job in the present, and it is what you do today and every day that creates the future you really want.

> Once you learn from your past bad experiences, forget them and focus on the present (today).

Learn from the past, and focus all your energy on the present. Each day's present becomes your future.

1. Stop replaying your past experiences and focus on the present.

2. If you replay any past experience, focus on what you can learn and then move on.

3. You can only ever accomplish anything in the present.

TRUTH

12

The size of your beliefs
determines the size of your
achievements

If your beliefs can drive what you can accomplish, then it goes without saying that the size of your beliefs will drive the size of your accomplishments. There's a great deal of power in that statement, and its impact on what you can accomplish in your life is just as powerful. If you are like most people, your self-belief might not be as big as what you want to accomplish. If what you want to accomplish is greater than your self-belief, then what you want is really more of a wish.

Dan Lier, "America's Coach", tells a great story which illustrates this concept of the size of your self-belief. To summarise the story here, Dan used to do training for one of the Tony Robbins companies and asked one of the very successful participants in his training group to have breakfast with him the next morning. Dan always liked to talk with successful people and learn more about how they became successful.

During the conversation, the successful participant made an interesting point to Dan. He said, "I don't really know what you want to do with your life or what you really want to achieve, but I can tell you one thing right now. I don't care how hard you work or what you do. You will never earn $250K a year with a $100K a year belief system you currently have in your head." That comment really hit Dan, and he found it absolutely right. In fact, Dan took what he learned and created the belief to become very successful.

> You can never accomplish beyond the belief that is inside you, and who controls what you believe? You do.

The numbers aren't as important as the difference in the numbers. You can never accomplish beyond the belief that is inside you, and who controls what you believe? You do. Donald Trump, US property tycoon, says, "As long as you're going to be thinking anyway, think big."

If you were to study the capabilities and skills of today's MBA graduates from the leading universities, you would find all of them with very similar capabilities and skills. So, what will make the difference in future years on what each of them will achieve?

If you could read their minds and understand the true beliefs in each of the graduates, you would see the difference. The size of the graduates' goals is always limited by the size of their beliefs, and the size of their beliefs is what is really driving the size of what they will accomplish.

You see many people investing time and money into their own education but often missing the belief that will really help them to utilise what they learn and achieve what they really want. Take a minute to think about that statement, and ask yourself, "Do I have the belief inside me to use the capabilities and skills I have to achieve what I want?"

You see, a belief is really a "sense of certainty". When your beliefs are weak, you have a low sense of certainty that you can really achieve what you want. When your beliefs are strong, you have a much higher sense of certainty that you can really achieve it.

If you have the capabilities and skills to achieve more than you are achieving today, the problem might not be in creating even greater capabilities and skills. The problem might be in the size of your beliefs, that sense of certainty that you can really accomplish it.

What's needed is to continually push the boundaries of your own beliefs, as the potential is inside you to accomplish almost anything you want. Your goal should be always to drive your beliefs to the size of your potential. Les Brown sums it up well, "People don't fail because they aim too high and miss, but because they aim too low and hit." Your beliefs will determine your aim, and thus your achievements.

> Your goal should be always to drive your beliefs to the size of your potential.

Your level of success begins with the level of your beliefs. No amount of activity will be enough if your beliefs are not big enough for the success you desire.

1. Always start by building the belief to the size of success you desire.
2. Aim high and grow your beliefs to achieve it.
3. Remember, a belief is really a sense of certainty.

TRUTH

13

Your attitude is really your window to the world

Your attitude is something that is completely within your control. When you leave your home each day, the attitude you enter the world with is entirely for you to choose. Enter the world with a good attitude, and it's like having a crystal clear windscreen in your car; you can see everything clearly and far into the distance. Your attitude is your window to your world.

There's a very good story that illustrates that your attitude is for you to choose. An elderly woman was changing retirement homes and was walking down the hallway with one of the attendants from the new home. The attendant was describing the room she would have, including the furnishings, colours of the walls, view from the window, etc. The older woman said, "I'll love it!" The attendant responded, "How can you say that, you haven't even seen the room yet?" At which the elderly woman replied, "My attitude towards the room and life is my choice. It is something I determine ahead of time."

Your attitude is a choice and is something you determine ahead of time. There are far too many people who let consequences or situations drive their attitude. If you are always letting consequences and other people determine your attitude, it is really as if you are surrendering leadership of your life to others. Never let outside circumstances or others determine how you should feel about yourself.

Sometimes more than any other factor, your attitude can determine what you will accomplish today, as your attitude is what can keep you positive and focused on the task at hand. However, your attitude is something that you can never just take for granted. To keep a positive attitude, you need to keep feeding it positive experiences.

> To keep a positive attitude, you need to keep feeding it positive experiences.

This is why you see many successful people often reading the same book over and over again, or listening to the same audios repeatedly. In fact, there are some very successful people who carry around with them everywhere the book that made the biggest impact on them, and changed their life. They are constantly re-

reading the book, and every time they read it, they gain even more insights and ideas.

There are two great outcomes for you to drive for yourself each and every day:

1. **Be the best you that you can be**—You know you have a great attitude when you can be the best *you* in any situation. There are so many people in the world who let others determine their attitude for them. Decide to be the best *you* in all situations.

2. **Be the person you would like to be around**—The other key outcome is to be the type of person you would like to be around, as this attitude will always attract others to help you.

> A great attitude is like a magnet and attracts the help of others.

No one accomplishes everything they want in life by themselves; it is always with the help of others. A great attitude is like a magnet and attracts the help of others. When you have a great attitude you will attract others to help you achieve the goals and outcomes you have defined for your life. Also, your attitude will determine the opportunities you see.

Your attitude is a choice. Choose to have a good attitude each and every day.

1. Choose your attitude and don't let others or circumstances determine it for you.

2. Keep your attitude positive and feed it positive experiences daily.

3. Your attitude shapes the way you see your world.

TRUTH

14

All actions begin in your thoughts first

What you accomplish (get done) begins in your mind first. You could say that the quality of your thoughts drives the quality of your actions. That being true, you could also say that the more quality thinking time you put into your life, the more you could get done. James Allen, author of *As a Man Thinketh*, said it best: "You are today where your thoughts have brought you; you will be tomorrow where your thoughts take you."

Many people go through life not really investing time in doing any quality thinking. If you think about it, you will always act out of habit if you never invest the time to think. Living a life based on your unchanged habits means that you would be doing the same things over and over again, and getting the same results.

If you were to drive your car across the grass, back and forth, over the same path each and every time, you would begin to create a rut. In fact, this is what you are doing to your own life if you do not invest the time for some quality thinking. Your habits would be simply driving you into a deeper and deeper rut.

In order to become better at getting the *right* things done, you need also to get better at doing your quality thinking. Most people would prefer to avoid thinking, as it can be challenging at times. However, as all your actions begin in your thoughts first, the quality of your thinking can determine the quality of your actions.

> In order to become better at getting the *right* things done, you need also to get better at doing your quality thinking.

Your thoughts enable you to take on life in a proactive way rather than in a reactive way. It is important to focus your thinking on what you want to accomplish and not simply on what you might need to do. This is all about looking at what you need to accomplish with an outcome focus. When you focus your quality thinking on outcomes, you will always see ideas on how to accomplish those outcomes with even fewer activities.

Do you have a time of day or times during your week set aside just to think? During these times when you are doing some quality thinking, you will begin to get some ideas on some key outcomes that you want to drive or even some specific actions that you need to take. Don't trust your memory and do take the time to write all these ideas down.

The most successful people are always writing down their thoughts, as they know that their thoughts are what are really driving their success. The more their thoughts are down on paper, the more possibilities there will be that they will drive action, and isn't action what it is all about?

> The most successful people are always writing down their thoughts.

David Allen, in his book *Getting Things Done: The Art of Stress-Free Productivity*, talks about the need to think in "next actions". It is very often that you think about what you need to do in too vague a way, and then never get to take action on your thoughts because of that. While you are doing your quality thinking and are thinking of some ideas to action, it is always good to think, right then and there, about the very next action that will move the idea forward. If you catch yourself being too vague about it, keep asking yourself the question, "What is the very next action?" David Allen says that your next actions are always something very simple, a call, an email, seeing someone, etc. When you break it down to the "rather simple" next action, you will have a much greater chance that you will actually do it.

Decide today how you will invest more time in doing more quality thinking. Set up times in your day and week to do some quality thinking on the key outcomes that will create the success you want. If you make it a habit, you will begin to see a change in your actions as well. Your quality of thinking will drive the quality of your actions, and what you will ultimately achieve.

Invest the time to do some quality thinking.

1. Set aside a specific time during the day just to think.
2. Capture down on paper all the ideas you think of.
3. Determine how to action those ideas right away— the next actions.

TRUTH

15

Positive thinking pushes out negative thinking

Positive thinking works and one of the biggest benefits is that when you have more positive thinking in your mind, there's not a great deal of room for any negative thinking. The people who stay positive are very good at filtering out the negative input and just focusing on the good.

It is really common sense, and you realise it for your own life. When you are positive, you physically feel much better and also find yourself taking more action. However, when you are negative in your thinking, you often find yourself not feeling well, and are likely to take less action (the opposite).

Why is it that the tendency of most people is to think about, often over and over again, the bad things that happen to them rather than the good things? All the negative news and what's happening in the world often makes you feel down. However, the majority of your "bad" thinking has nothing to do with the outside world, but what you manufacture in your mind all by yourself.

As mentioned above, you tend to take less action when you are not feeling positive. If you want to become better at getting things done, keeping yourself thinking positive can be a very beneficial thing to do.

Sometimes you don't necessarily need to think positive. Just by eliminating the negative thinking from your daily life allows what's left to move towards more positive thinking.

Jerry Clark, on his programme *Think Like a Giant* on www.tstn.com and www.clubrhino.com, talks about a

> Just by eliminating the negative thinking from your daily life allows what's left to move towards more positive thinking.

great idea, a Mental Fast. Jerry suggests that you take a break, a fast, from all the negative news you get from TV and newspapers. Why not take a month and decide to avoid all the negative news you see on TV and read in the newspapers? It is often the negative input you allow into your mind that consumes your thoughts and doesn't allow the positive thinking ever to enter. By eliminating the negative, and without the negative input going into your brain, you will naturally become more positive. This is a great way of filtering out the bad and focusing on the good.

At the same time, you have more time to invest in your own personal development and read books or listen to audios that will help you grow and stay positive. The most successful people and the greatest achievers are constantly feeding their minds positive experiences. They treat these positive experiences as if they were food for success, and just as you would not last very long without food, they feel that their success will not last for ever unless they are constantly feeding themselves positive experiences that will continue to inspire their action.

> To stay positive each and every day, you need to fill your mind with the positive each and every day.

Staying positive and motivated is not something that you can take for granted. Your personal development and filling your mind with positive readings is not something you can do just once in a while. To stay positive each and every day, you need to fill your mind with the positive each and every day.

Remember, it is all about filling your mind with positive input. This comes from what you read, what you listen to, and the people you spend your time with. When you fill your mind with positive input and begin to think more positive thoughts, you will not leave any room for the negative thoughts any more.

Strive to fill your mind with the positive, and you will find yourself with more motivation each day to take the necessary actions and accomplish what you want in your life.

Stay positive and keep yourself in the best mindset for action.

1. Push out negative thinking by filling your mind with positive input and experiences.

2. Positive thinking fuels your motivation to take more action.

3. There's never any room for negative thinking if you constantly fill your mind with the positive.

TRUTH

16

What you learn only has power when put into action

You can never learn enough in your life if you just rely on your own experiences. What you read and listen to and the people you meet can have a big impact on what you learn and what you are then capable of accomplishing. However, what you learn only has power when it is put into action.

If just learning new things would help us succeed faster, then all the libraries around the world would be packed. What you learn is important, but what action you take on what you learn will be what creates the success you desire.

> Moving what you learn to action is what it is all about.

Moving what you learn to action is what it is all about.

You learn in two ways:

1. **Through your self-development**—Your self-development is all about the books you read, the audios you listen to, or the education videos/quality TV programmes you watch. Successful people are life-long learners. They know that their self-development is what is going to move them ahead in life and is a critical part of reaching their goals and the success they desire. It is the same for you.

   Your achievements and your ability to get things done are often directly proportional to how big you grow yourself, and your own self-development plan is a major part of it.

   What you learn is not enough. Remember, it is about putting it into action, and here's a tip to use during your self-development: whenever you do your self-development and read, listen to or watch something interesting, stop yourself and ask the following question: "How can I apply this to my life?"

   When you hear something interesting and don't think more about it, you file it away into your brain in just a *that's interesting* category. This might contain some useful information for you, but you didn't really think at the time how you might be able to use it. Why not include one extra step in your self-development?

Ask yourself: "How can I apply this to my life?" If you answer this question, and think about the possible ways you could use what you learned, then what you are really doing is moving it from a *that's interesting* category to an *action* category in your brain.

Your brain will associate what you have learned with the possible ways you would apply it (the actions), and store it that way. You will then see the power behind this in the future. When you encounter an experience that matches what you learned and the way you could apply it, your brain will offer up the possible actions to you (just like magic). Why? Because you have stored what you learned in an *action* way rather than in just a *that's interesting* way.

Why not try this during your own self-development, and you will store what you learned in your brain in an *action* way?

2. **Through your experiences in life**—The second way you learn is from the experiences you have in your life. These come from all the interactions you have during your daily life and from the key relationships you build with others.

    You can apply a similar tip as described above with self-development, and ask yourself the following question after key experiences you have each day: "What did I learn from this experience and how can I apply this to my life?"

    It is just one question, but it can make the difference between your using what you learned from your daily experiences in the future or not.

Always asking yourself "How can I apply this to my life?" will help you put what you learned into action and get more things done in the future.

Take what you learn into action:

1. Through your self-development: "How can I apply this to my life?"

2. Through your experiences in life: "What did I learn from this experience and how can I apply it to my life?"

3. You get more done when you apply what you learn.

TRUTH

17

Be proactive, not reactive, by thinking ahead

There is an old saying, "If you fail to plan, you plan to fail." That is really true and your ability to get things done comes down to whether you take a proactive or reactive approach to life. Everyone achieves more when they take a more proactive approach to life and think ahead in order to get more accomplished.

For many people, life just seems to keep sneaking up on them. They are going through life reacting to everything that hits them, and then wondering why they are not getting anything done that they wanted to do. Because they are just reacting to everyone else, they are just doing what everyone else wants them to do. Does this situation sound familiar to you? Do you feel that you are doing more of what others want than what you really want?

With such a fast pace to life today, you really need to think ahead and make sure you schedule your week in such a way that you get to achieve what you want to achieve, not doing only what others want you to do. Thinking ahead makes you proactive rather than reactive.

This upfront thinking time is when you remind yourself of what is most important to you and then you refine your focus for the coming week. You could say that your most important thinking activity is to be continually refining your focus. Remember, it is all about focus management, not time management. The time you invest in both creating and maintaining your focus will pay you 10 times over in you being more productive and getting more done during your week.

Also, your time spent thinking ahead is when you do your quality thinking on the key outcomes you would like to accomplish. These are the key outcomes that will take you closer to what you want, and will drive your actions to accomplish them. You may recall, Noah didn't wait to build the ark until after the rain started. He made a plan ahead of time and then took the action.

> Your time spent thinking ahead is when you do your quality thinking on the key outcomes you would like to accomplish.

Thinking ahead not only helps you to be more productive, but also enables you to get more help from others. When you think ahead, you usually have more time to arrange the help of others to accomplish more of what you want to achieve. Getting things done is always a factor in what you need to do and also what help you can get from others. The think ahead time helps you create a plan of action that gets the most done by utilising both yourself and others in the most productive ways possible.

Lastly, thinking ahead enables you to quickly refocus how you use your time when the priorities change. Many people talk about multi-tasking, but what you are really doing is just one task at a time. What really is happening is rapid refocusing. Planning ahead allows you to have thought everything through in advance, and this enables you to move quickly from one task to another (rapid refocusing).

Most of the very productive people you see are very good at rapid refocusing. Their investment in thinking ahead has enabled them to understand very well what needs to get done, and to know how they will accomplish it, because it has been planned ahead of time. This allows them to refocus themselves from one task to another, and very quickly. Why? Because they have already thought through what to do, they don't have to think through what to do each time they change the task. They only have to refocus the mind to the new task, and this gets them quickly into the action.

You can do the same for yourself. Invest the time up front to think through the key actions you need to take and you will become a master at rapid refocusing as well. The more you master rapid refocusing, the more you will get done, each and every day.

> The more you master rapid refocusing, the more you will get done, each and every day.

Thinking and planning ahead helps you focus your time to accomplish more.

1. Thinking ahead helps you plan better actions.
2. Thinking and planning ahead enables you to schedule your time more productively.
3. Thinking ahead enables rapid refocusing.

TRUTH
18

Planning drives faster decisions and action

In reality, a plan is outdated the minute it has been completed, as the world is moving so fast these days. However, the very act of creating a plan forces you to think through what you want to accomplish in such detail that it provides you with a great understanding to make faster decisions as you take action on it.

When you plan ahead and think things through in advance, you often think about the possible situations that you might encounter and what the possible implications could be. This leads you to think about your own options in addressing any of the possibilities, and this helps you to be much better prepared. By driving your thinking and planning deeper and broader on the subject, you develop a much better understanding about what you want to accomplish and the different options you have to achieve it.

This understanding is very valuable as you go through each day and week. You only really have to integrate the newest information with that which you have already thought through, and this enables you to make faster decisions. Your upfront thinking and planning has given you a more complete understanding, and this provides you with the confidence to make faster decisions and take action quicker.

You often see leaders with the ability to understand complex topics quickly and make those fast decisions. When you see this, you get quite impressed and think they are very intelligent, as they are able to understand these complex topics very quickly. However, it is often the case that they are really no more intelligent than many others. It is just that they invested the time to do their upfront planning and thought everything through on the topics and in some detail ahead of time. This allows them to integrate any new information very quickly and respond just as fast. So can you!

Your ability to make decisions faster and with more confidence can become a major factor in your getting more things done. How many times have you put off deciding something, and because you didn't take any decision, you were also not taking any action? You have never seen a successful person who had trouble taking decisions. Why? Because successful people know that decisions are what keeps the action going, and that delaying decisions means delaying action.

Investing in the upfront planning and thinking is what can enable you to think through the decisions that are coming up in your week, and it enables you to do some quality thinking and understanding of the key factors and information that will drive those decisions. What is important is to set aside the time to invest in the upfront planning and thinking.

Your ability to make decisions faster and with more confidence can become a major factor in your getting more things done.

The most successful people block off at least 30 minutes each week to think ahead to the possible decisions that they will need to make that week. This is when they actually decide whether they will need any further information, and if they do, they request it right away. Think back in your own life, and you will think of many times when you were uncomfortable taking a fast decision simply because you did not feel you had all the information. This planning and thinking ahead helps you uncover that missing information sooner, and allows you to make your decisions faster.

Planning and thinking ahead enables you to take faster decisions.

1. Thinking things through in advance helps you to reach conclusions faster.

2. Your upfront thinking enables you to integrate any new information quickly.

3. You will always be better prepared than others because you invested time in thinking ahead.

TRUTH

19

You can't wait for the inspiration to take action

Do you ever put off the things that you know you should be doing? If you are like others, you probably procrastinate more than you would like to. Procrastination is always putting off what you can do today, or what you could even do right now, to later on. When you procrastinate on what's most important to you, then what you are really doing is pushing your *future* further into the future.

Successful people are very action oriented and don't wait for the inspiration to take the necessary actions. They have their goals that they want to achieve, and they stay focused on those goals all the time. For these successful people, they know that if they take the necessary actions, the inspiration will then come along to help them complete them.

> Successful people are very action oriented and don't wait for the inspiration to take the necessary actions.

How many times have you put off an important task because you just didn't feel like doing it, or because it was a rather difficult one and you thought you didn't know where to start? In fact, you may have put that task off for days, weeks or even months.

A great example of this is completing your tax return. You look at it as difficult or time consuming, and you just don't feel the inspiration to start it. However, once you have started on the work, the inspiration comes to finish it, and it actually takes a lot less time than you originally thought. So, the inspiration came to you to finish it, but only after you took the action to get the task started.

Successful people are very action oriented and expect the inspiration will come to finish the task once they start it. They expect to get the feeling to do it only after they have actually started the task. This really is the opposite for unsuccessful people. Unsuccessful people have to feel like doing it before taking any action on the task.

You could summarise the difference with the following definitions of both successful people and unsuccessful people:

- Successful people let their behaviours drive their feelings.
- Unsuccessful people let their feelings drive their behaviours.

Do you see the difference?

Unsuccessful people go through life always waiting for the inspiration, and only take action when they feel like it. Successful people are just the opposite. They are constantly taking action and very often make many more mistakes than the unsuccessful people ever do. However, the successful people are always moving forward by taking the action, while the unsuccessful people just stay still.

How about another example? Let's take the example of what happens to many sales people. Sales people often have to talk to many potential customers until they find one who will buy. Every time a potential customer says "no", the sales person gets a negative feeling, and maybe that negative feeling gets even bigger with every no the sales person receives. Very soon, the sales person starts to delay (procrastinate) calling potential customers, and calls fewer potential customers each day. If you were this sales person, what do you think would happen to the level of sales you would make if you called fewer and fewer people each day? You would get such a negative feeling every time you heard a no, that you would call potential customers less and less to avoid the feeling of rejection (the no's). You would be letting your feelings drive your behaviours.

Your life today is the result of the choices and actions that you have taken up to this point. If you procrastinate on those actions that are important to achieve the life you want, then you are really pushing the life you want further into the future.

However, you can do what you need to do every day, and achieve what you want in your life, if you just remind yourself of the following each and every day:

1. Don't wait for the inspiration to take action.
2. Let your behaviours drive your feelings.
3. If you wait to take action, you will be behind the others who don't wait.

TRUTH

20

What you do today creates your future

Right now, can you take action in the past? No, it is gone for ever. Can you take action in the future? Yes, but that means you would be putting off any action until later, procrastinating. The only way to create a different future for yourself is to take action *today, now.*

Accomplishing what you want in your life is all about what you do today, and every day from this day forward. John Wooden, a very successful US college basketball coach, said it best: "Make today your masterpiece."

Your actions today create the future you want, and whatever you don't do today is really pushing your future further into the future. Remember, your past is gone and it can only be useful for learning how to do things better, both today and into the future. The future is not here yet, and is determined by what you do today, and today is the time for getting things done.

The key is to focus all your energy on what you can accomplish today. You need to think big about what you want to accomplish (the outcomes), but small on the daily actions needed

The key is to focus all your energy on what you can accomplish today.

to achieve them. The most successful people always focus on the actions they can take each and every day that will move them closer to the goals they want to achieve. Remember, these successful people always have the big dreams, goals and outcomes in their mind, but they break those down to the necessary daily actions that will help them achieve them.

What you do each and every day is really based on your habits. In fact, most of what you do each day is driven more by habit than by thought. If what you do today creates your future, and your habits are what are essentially driving your actions each day, then it makes sense that a great place to start in getting more done each day is with your habits.

A great question to ask yourself is whether or not your current daily habits are helping you make the most of each and every day. If your current daily habits are not helping you, then think about what you would need to do differently.

For most people, the missing daily habits and actions are most related to discipline, or to be more specific, the lack of discipline.

Why not ask yourself: "In which daily habits am I lacking the discipline to do the necessary actions that will move me closer to my goals?"

As with everything else, the key is getting the answers to this question out of your head and down on paper. You would see a difference in what you accomplish each day if you were to:

1. Write down a list of daily habits and the discipline you need to put into them.

2. Make the decision to review this list four times day—at breakfast, lunch, dinner, and right before bed.

The very act of reviewing this list of habits and discipline will drive you to take action on them. By reminding yourself at times when you are already doing something (i.e. meal times, etc.), there should be no excuse for not doing this review.

Remember, what you accomplish each day is driven by what you put into your focus. The more you remind yourself of your focus (especially those daily habits), the more you will *do it*.

> The more you remind yourself of your focus, the more you will *do it*.

Action can only happen in the present, and the sum of your todays equals your future.

1. Focus on getting the most out of each and every day.

2. It is what you do today that creates your future.

3. Put those habits in place that help you make the most of each and every day.

21

Discipline is doing what's necessary, when it is necessary

You can have the best ideas, define the right outcomes, and have your plans all in place. That's great. However, you will also need to create in yourself the discipline to do what is necessary, when it is necessary. Everyone is great at being motivated or disciplined to do what he or she likes, but for you to truly get things done, you will need to do what's necessary as well. Thomas Edison said, "The successful person makes a habit of doing what the failing person doesn't like to do."

The speaker and author Jim Cathcart created a great question: "How would the person I'd like to be, do the things I am about to do?" After one of his speaking events, one of the participants asked Jim if he had any slogan or saying that could be used to motivate himself every day. Jim said he didn't have any slogan, but offered the participant that question.

The key is doing what's necessary, but necessary for what? The *what* is really the success you defined both for what you want to achieve and for the lifestyle you would like to have. The *necessary* is what you need to do each and every day that takes you closer to what you want. Jim Cathcart's question is one of the best ways both to focus on what's necessary and to motivate yourself to do it.

"How would the person I'd like to be, do the things I am about to do?"

The discipline to do what's necessary is very much powered by the *why* behind what you want. To become successful and achieve what you want, you will often have to do what's necessary, and when it is necessary, and even the tasks you really don't like to do. The difference

> **The discipline to do what's necessary is very much powered by the *why* behind what you want.**

between successful and unsuccessful people is often just that. Successful people are willing to do what unsuccessful people are unwilling to do.

The *will* to do it is driven by the *why*. A *why* has to be powerful enough to provide the *will* to do what's necessary. If you find yourself not doing what you know you should be doing, then go back and build the *why* bigger behind what you want.

The *why* powers you to do the necessary. Build your *why* big enough so that it will power you to do the necessary, when it is necessary.

If you are like others, you are always putting off those tasks you really should be doing, and they are the very ones that will take you closer to what you want. You could call those tasks your necessary evils. To you, they are evil, as you seem always to be avoiding them. However, these "evils" are the very tasks that you absolutely need to do.

One idea is always to focus first on those necessary tasks that you really don't like to do. If you build the drive to do those first in your day, the rest of the day becomes much easier, as you then begin to do all the other tasks you enjoy doing. Just by doing all those necessary evils first, you will accomplish more each and every day.

Just by doing all those necessary evils first, you will accomplish more each and every day.

Why not make a list of those necessary tasks, and put the list in a place where it will be reminding you each and every day?

Focus on doing the "necessary" first each and every day.

The discipline to do the *necessary* is the foundation for success.

1. It's either the pain of discipline, or the pain of regret.
2. The *why* creates the power and discipline to do the necessary.
3. You have never seen an undisciplined successful person.

22

You create your habits and
your habits create you

What you do each and every day and what you accomplish is based a great deal on your habits. They often say that you can tell how successful a person will be just by looking at their habits. If this is the case, then it is really true that you create your habits and then your habits create you.

People are doing this all the time. They keep doing the same things (the habits), but expect different results. You can never really accomplish anything great in your life without changing your habits first.

> You can never really accomplish anything great in your life without changing your habits first.

Experts say that it takes at least 28 days to establish a new habit. Establishing a habit means to repeat it often enough that you have taken what was uncomfortable to you and have made it comfortable.

You cannot really change your life, and get more of the *right* things done, unless you change your habits. If each and every day you do the same things, then you have to expect the same results. Albert Einstein defined this as "Insanity: doing the same thing over and over again and expecting different results".

If you want different results, then you need to decide what habits you need to create. If you make the commitment to change your habits, and stick with it for at least 28 days, then you have the way to create different results.

Here's a great example of making something a real habit from Jerry Seinfeld, the comedian. Jerry knew that success for him was in writing better jokes, and the way to create better jokes was to write every day. He had a technique he used on himself and you can use it to motivate yourself—even when you don't feel like it. His technique involved using a unique calendar system to drive himself to write. Here's how it works:

Jerry had a calendar that had a whole year on one page, and a red marker. Each day that he wrote, he put a big red X over that day. Jerry explained, "After a few days you'll have a chain. Just keep at it and the chain will grow longer every day. You'll like seeing that chain, especially when you get a few weeks under your belt. Your only job next is to not break the chain." "Don't break the chain," Jerry said again for emphasis.

Why not begin a chain for the key habit that would make the most difference in your life? In fact, most people are only one or two key habits away from really becoming successful in their chosen career. However, these habits are more often related to a person's character than to any other abilities that they might have. If

Most people are only one or two key habits away from really becoming successful in their chosen career.

you were to study the core character traits of successful people, you would notice two key character traits that all of them possess.

They are **discipline** and **commitment**.

All successful people have made the commitment to themselves to take whatever action is necessary for them to achieve their goals. Their commitment is visible to others by the discipline they have and by the habits they have put into their daily lives in order to guarantee that those actions are being done.

You can see that the habits are what are making these successful people so successful. They have created the habits, and their habits have created their success.

You can do the same. If you create the *right* habits, your habits will create you and the success you desire.

Focus on your habits and your habits will enable your success.

1. Your habits are the foundation for your actions.
2. Your daily actions are what creates the success you desire.
3. You create your habits and then your habits will create you.

TRUTH

23

That little bit extra makes a huge difference

Look at the sports world and the famous 100 m races at the Olympics. The difference between the winner and second place is often just a couple of hundredths of a second. The winner was only just a little bit faster, but it made a huge difference in the result, as usually nobody remembers who came second in the race.

What do you think contributed to that little difference in time, but a big difference in the result? Very often, it has come down to that little bit extra the winner did in preparation for the race. Maybe an extra 15 minutes stretching every day, skipping those unhealthy foods that he or she loved, or maybe even some small differences in the preparation done the day before the race.

Many people think there is always a big difference between first and second place, both in sports and in life. However, it is almost always that little bit extra that creates the big difference. The difference between first and second is often just that little extra bit of discipline that's inside the one and not the other.

> The difference between first and second is often just that little extra bit of discipline that's inside the one and not the other.

Think about your own life and how you prepare for meetings at work. Often the difference between a successful and an unsuccessful meeting is whether the preparation was done or not. In fact, that preparation is usually not taking much time, but if you didn't discipline yourself to do it, it wouldn't get done. This little extra preparation can make all the difference between a successful meeting and an unsuccessful one.

How about another example? Sales people understand that the more they know about a customer, the better the questions they can ask in uncovering the customer's true needs, and whether their products and services can really help the customer. However, most sales people do not always do their preparation, and it often requires just a little extra investment of time in order to look up on the internet some information on the customer and the company they will be visiting. Also, for sales people, it is often that one extra sales call that they make each day, and this is often something that other sales people are either not able or not willing to fit into their schedule.

If you were to think about similar situations in your own life, you would certainly be able to think of countless situations where that little bit extra could have made a big difference for you. The key is to develop the discipline to always give that little bit extra. If you do, you will differentiate yourself from those who won't, and this is often the majority of the others.

There's a very basic concept that really highlights this point. If you do what everyone else is doing, by default, you are just one of the crowd. It is very difficult to do that little extra and really set yourself apart from the others if you are constantly staying with the crowd. Why not separate yourself from the crowd and determine to do that little bit extra that will set you apart?

> **Why not separate yourself from the crowd and determine to do that little bit extra that will set you apart?**

Setting a goal of giving a little bit extra every day could have a tremendous impact on your life and the success you will achieve. That little bit extra is almost never in the difficult tasks, but in the easy tasks that are often difficult to do (the ones requiring that little extra discipline to do).

Give that little bit extra that others are not willing to do.

1. A little extra every day can create the difference.
2. Strive to do what others are unwilling to do.
3. Make it a habit to do that little bit extra.

24

People really don't fail, they just stop taking action

If you talk to successful entrepreneurs, they can always tell you about the critical time when things were going badly and everyone else thought that they should quit. Well, they didn't quit and kept taking action, as they had the belief that if they just kept at it long enough they would be successful.

A great example of this is the life of the US President, Abraham Lincoln. He is remembered for his leadership during one of the most difficult times in United States history, the civil war period. Abraham Lincoln experienced many setbacks in his life. Actually, he experienced more setbacks than many of you could experience in many lifetimes. Just to give you a little summary, Abraham Lincoln failed in two businesses, lost over seven elections, and experienced a total nervous breakdown. Yet, he went on to become the President of the United States because he kept taking action. He never quit.

Many people stop just short of success because they just quit. If you read the biographies of successful entrepreneurs you will find that many times they could have easily failed if they stopped taking action. Many of them faced at least one challenge in their lives when it looked as if nothing could be done to overcome it. However, they didn't quit and kept taking action until they worked their way through the challenges.

Everyone encounters challenges to overcome in their lives, and these challenges are always helping you to grow stronger as well. The difference is that successful people have the perseverance to keep taking action, no matter what types of challenges they face. They have the belief inside them that they will be able to meet any challenge or solve any problem that comes their way.

Look again at the example of Abraham Lincoln. He could have quit running for office and just given up on life with all the troubles he encountered. In fact, you see many people giving up on life today and they have faced only a fraction of the challenges that Abraham Lincoln faced. However, he kept strong in what he wanted to contribute in his life and just kept taking action.

You only really become a failure when you stop taking action. The people who achieve success in their lives have perseverance. They will stick with what's important to them because they have the belief in themselves that they will ultimately accomplish it.

Everyone has problems in their lives, and the bigger the goals you would like to accomplish, the bigger the problems will be for you to solve. There are many people who think the opposite, that the more success they achieve, the easier will be the problems they will encounter. You will always have problems or challenges in your life in equal proportion to the goals you set for yourself.

The people who achieve success in their lives have perseverance.

The difference between the successful and the unsuccessful people is all about how they view the problems and their approach to them. Pastor and author Robert H. Schuller said it best: "Problems are not stop signs; they are guidelines." The people who look at problems as stop signs are always giving up too soon, and often at the very step where their success would be just starting for them, if only they kept at it.

People who don't quit have perseverance. Perseverance comes from the belief that they will do it. So can you. You really only fail when you fail to keep taking action.

Failure only comes when you have given up.

1. You only ever fail when you stop taking action.
2. Success comes when you don't give up when others do.
3. Action is the way to face any challenge or problem.

TRUTH

25

It is easier to create a new habit than break an old one

If you are like others, you have habits that you wish you didn't have. Also, if you are like many others, you have probably tried to break the habit several times, and with no success. To break a habit you have to continually think about not doing it, and always think about the very thing you would like to stop. Does that sound like a great way for you to break a habit, by having to constantly think about what you don't want to do?

In fact, it is often that several of your old habits are what are preventing you from becoming better at getting things done. A far easier approach is to create a new habit that could replace the old one. If you just focused on the creation of the new habit, you would be focusing your mind on something positive, creating something new, not on something negative, stopping something you shouldn't be doing.

There are many examples of this that you have seen in other people's lives and maybe even in your own.

Take the example of people who would like to quit smoking. Smoking also has an addictive part to it, but often the problem is that people need to continually remind themselves not to smoke. Many of the people who have successfully quit have replaced the smoking habit with something else. Some, when they felt the urge for a smoke, just went on a short walk.

The same is true for people who want to lose weight. The people who are always focused on what they shouldn't eat are never really successful at staying on their diet and losing the weight they want. The successful people are those who have decided on a completely different diet, rather than trying to cut down on something they are used to and like.

The important point is that people who replace old habits with new ones are far more successful at having these new habits stick.

People who replace old habits with new ones are far more successful at having these new habits stick.

The above examples are all about creating a new habit rather than trying either to stop or to reduce an old one. Those examples were something big, like quitting smoking or losing weight. However, there are many very small habits that you do, day in and day out, which are not helping you to get what you want.

Always ask yourself the following question about the habits you currently have: "Do my habits help me to get closer to what I want to achieve and the life I want to live or not?" Ask this question for each habit, and if the habit is not helping you to get closer to what you want, then it is a target to be replaced.

Next, for all the habits that are not taking you closer to what you want to achieve in your life, think about the *right* habits you could replace those habits with. Remember, everything in our lives first begins in our thoughts. This investment of time in thinking through your habits could lead you to put into your life those one or two new habits that will drive your future success.

To break an old habit, focus on creating a new one instead, and replace that old one.

It is much easier to replace a habit than to just stop an old habit.

1. Always think about replacing an old/bad habit with a new one.

2. Focusing on the new is always a better approach than focusing on stopping the old.

3. Replacing is always easier than thinking about stopping.

26

You achieve better rapport
by adapting your approach
to others

Your life is all about relationships, both the professional and personal ones. The more you create rapport with others, the more you feel you trust them and the more they trust you. If you think about it, do you act exactly the same way when you are with all your friends? Maybe not, and you might have learned about how to create better rapport with any new people you meet, both the professional and personal ones.

You all know the golden rule: "Do unto others as you would have them do unto you." Well, Dr Tony Alessandra, speaker and author, developed The Platinum Rule®, which is "Do unto others as they would like to be done unto." Tony has highlighted the key to building better rapport with others. People don't really want to be treated the way you would like to be treated. They want to be treated the way they like to be treated.

> People don't really want to be treated the way you would like to be treated. They want to be treated the way they like to be treated.

It is far too often that people expect others to like what they like and react to the world in the very same way. However, it just doesn't work that way. Everyone has different personalities and has grown up with different experiences, and to be successful in your communications, you need both to understand this and to adapt your approach.

This can be illustrated by using the analogy of a hamburger. There are some people who are tremendously focused and don't want any small talk (the bun) with their conversations with others. They want only the facts (the meat), and usually keep any small talk to an absolute minimum.

However, there are others who will not listen to the facts (the meat), without first engaging in small talk. They would feel uncomfortable if someone started the conversation right away with the facts (the meat) and didn't engage in any small talk at all.

You really need to construct the hamburger of conversations in a different way for everyone you meet. By adapting your approach to the other person's preferred style of communicating, you will create greater rapport. When you create greater rapport, you will get the other person to listen more closely to what you are saying. In fact, communication is never an outcome. It is only an activity. It is all about having the other person understanding you and doing what you want. That is the desired outcome.

> By adapting your approach to the other person's preferred style of communicating, you will create greater rapport.

How about an example? Many bosses experience this problem with some of their people. Bosses tend to be extremely driven and focused on getting things done. Also, they are usually busy, and in all their conversations, they tend to get right to the point and begin right with the facts (the meat). However, they always have some employees in their organisation who get nervous when speaking to their boss, and often are not listening very closely at the beginning of any conversation. If the boss gets right to the facts (the meat) with this type of person, there's a good chance that they won't be listening very clearly at the beginning of the conversation. The better approach for the boss would be to engage in some small talk (the bun) to put the other person at ease, before talking about the details (the meat).

The same problem often happens in reverse. The employee comes into the boss talking about the weather, etc., and lots of other small talk (the bun), and the boss becomes more frustrated every second this continues. The boss wants to get right down to business (the meat) and finds all that small talk a waste of time.

In both these situations between the boss and the employee, they would have much better interactions if each were trying to adapt to the other.

So can you. The more you adapt to others, the more they will adapt to you.

Adapt your approach to others for greater success.

1. Treat people as they would like to be treated.
2. Adapt your approach to build greater rapport.
3. Before every conversation, think about how you need to construct the *hamburger*.

TRUTH

27

Remove the emotions first
and then discuss the facts

In your life you will always encounter people who get emotional over an issue, and you either deal with it or run from it. Of course, the best approach is to deal with it, but in the right way. People who get emotional will want to express it, and not listen to your logic or the facts, and understanding this can make a big difference.

People who get emotional will always want the opportunity to share what they are feeling first, before engaging in other discussions. It is important for you to acknowledge what they are feeling and their concerns, and to be a very good listener to what they have to say. In many ways, it is all about the follow-up questions you ask that makes others feel that you are both interested and listening, and that you really want to understand what they are feeling.

People who get emotional will always want the opportunity to share what they are feeling first, before engaging in other discussions.

There are too many people who try to use logic and the facts to argue a point with someone who is already emotional. This never works, as the emotional person is not in the mood to listen, and is in fact just in the mood to share what they are feeling. During these times, there is no use in trying to share any more information, as it will never help the situation, and will probably only make it worse.

This is the time simply to listen, and to ask questions that will allow the other person to share completely their thoughts and what they are feeling. Until the other person has shared their feelings, and to the level that makes them feel more at ease or comfortable, you should never try to share any more information from your side.

The goal here is to remove the emotions first. Once you have allowed the other person to share completely their thoughts and emotions, then and only then can you begin by sharing your information and the facts behind the issue. Listening to the other person's feelings will then "earn" you the right with them to share your information.

Unfortunately, this is not always the way people treat these situations. How many times have you become emotional on an issue and the other person was just trying to convince you with all the facts and information as to why they knew they were right? I would guess that after the first few facts you stopped listening and this only increased the level of emotions on both sides of the issue.

Also, you might have experienced the opposite when you were dealing with an issue and the other person was getting emotional. You might have thought that it is best to stick to the facts and the information, and take the emotion out of the argument. The more you shared the facts, information and logic behind the issue, the more emotional the other person became. What happened is that you didn't allow the other person to share their feelings before you shared your information.

As you can see with these examples, you always need to remove the emotions first, and then discuss the facts. The main reason why people don't do this is pressure on time and the lack of patience. Most people feel that they don't have the time just to listen to others' thoughts and feelings, and their lack of patience drives them to force the issue more quickly and with more facts and information.

> You always need to remove the emotions first, and then discuss the facts.

To become more effective in dealing with emotional situations and on difficult issues, always be patient and invest the time to listen to the other person's thoughts and feelings. Almost always, once you have listened, you will then "earn" the right, from the other person, to share your side (the facts).

Remember to remove the emotions first and then discuss the facts.

Others will not listen to you until they have been able to share how they are feeling.

1. Be prepared to listen before sharing what you want them to know.

2. Listening and empathising first earns you the right to share your information.

3. Have the *patience* to listen.

TRUTH

28

You are in "sales", as you are always selling your ideas to others

Talk to anyone about sales people, and you will get either a very positive or a very negative reaction. No one ever seems to be very neutral on the topic of sales people. However, you and others should be very positive about sales, as you are all in sales. You might not be in the selling profession as a sales person, but you are in your own selling profession of selling yourself and your ideas.

Everyone is in sales, as everyone needs to sell themselves to others. How you communicate and package your key messages can make a big difference in what you are able to achieve and the help you can get from others. You are really selling your ideas and the value you can bring to others around you. The more value they see in working with you, the more help you will get from them in achieving what you want as well.

There are far too many people who first think about what others need to understand from them. They are constantly focusing on the information they need to share and end up sharing far too much, and this results in really boring people. To be more effective in selling your ideas to others, it is better to focus first on being more persuasive than informative.

> To be more effective in selling your ideas to others, it is better to focus first on being more persuasive than informative.

Selling is all about buying, and getting others to understand your ideas and the value you can bring to them. To understand selling, you really need to understand buying, as you need first to get others to buy into what you are saying.

People first need to buy into your ideas, before they buy into you.

As with sales, the most important thing is to focus your communications on the other person. What is the other person interested in, and what would they want to hear? Also, think about what you want the other person to understand and feel about what you want to say.

The focus of all good communications is first on who you are communicating to, and second on what you want to communicate.

By focusing on whom you are communicating to, you think ahead on what you will say and how it will be interpreted, and this enables you to tailor your communications to meet their expectations.

Selling your ideas and selling yourself is never about having the focus on you. It is all about placing the focus on the other person and how you can help him or her with what they want. By helping others get what they want, you will always get their attention and bring the focus back to you in return.

> Selling your ideas and selling yourself is never about having the focus on you.

Remember, you are always selling your ideas to others and this is what enables you to get help in achieving what you want in life.

1. To understand selling, understand buying. It is how others will receive what you say.

2. The ability to influence others (selling) is a fundamental skill for success.

3. You are in sales, as you are always selling your ideas to others.

29

Questions have more power than answers

Two people are having a conversation together. One is asking all the questions and the other is providing all the answers. Which person is in control of the conversation? It's the questions that have more power than the answers, as the questions control the conversation.

Questions help you to control the conversations with other people, and this helps you to focus those conversations more on what helps you to get what you want. If you are not asking the questions in your conversations with others, then others are controlling the conversations and focusing the discussions on what they want rather than what you want.

Questions are also very powerful in building relationships. Questions show that you are interested in what others have to say. By showing interest in others, others will show interest in you. Also, questions have the power to influence others. How? Because questions help others to think, and think about something they never realised before. You gain more influence with others by asking them questions that make them think than you do by just providing them with answers.

Questions are the fuel that enables you to tailor communication and key messages to others. You always have more effective conversations when you get others talking first. They share their thoughts and information with you that will enable you to "package" your thoughts and ideas back to them by using their words and not yours.

> **Questions are the fuel that enables you to tailor communication and key messages to others.**

Everyone shares their ideas and explains things in different ways and with different words. Asking questions up front to uncover these differences then allows you to match others' ways and words in sharing your own ideas back to them. This helps you to get your ideas understood faster by others.

If you are a leader, questions are what help your people to think through the solutions, rather than you just providing them with the answers. Every time you provide answers to your people, you are taking back a little bit of the ownership of the solution, as they will be executing your solution based on your answers, and not theirs.

Questions have the power to help people see the answers on their own, thus keeping the ownership of executing the solution driven by their answers, not yours. You could say that questions are like an investment of time for leaders, as they get their people thinking and developing the answers on their own. However, providing answers is just the opposite, and is as if you are spending time, as you have saved your people from thinking (and growing).

You can also see the power of questions in sales. The old saying goes, "If the customer is talking, you are winning. If you are talking, you are losing." Questions get others talking and sharing more of their

> **Questions show interest, and interest drives influence.**

ideas and information with you. When you understand others better, you have the "fuel" to influence others better as well. Questions show interest, and interest drives influence.

Why not do a mini-review after all the conversations you had this week? Ask yourself: "How was my questions to answers ratio?" Or you could phrase the question: "How was my listen versus talk ratio?"

In all your interactions and conversations with others, questions have more power than answers.

Questions put you in control of conversations.

1. Questions have the power to influence others. They get them thinking!
2. Questions show your interest in others.
3. Questions keep others with the ownership.

TRUTH
30

Stories and examples make the emotional link faster

If you look at the best speakers, they are usually also the best storytellers. Great speakers are telling stories, providing examples and linking any information in their talks to these stories and examples. They know that stories and examples get people more involved in the talk, as everyone is paying attention and trying to follow the story or example.

To get the help of others, you often first need to grab their attention and get them to listen to you closely, and to what you have to say. More than any other communication idea, the use of stories and examples will make the emotional link with others faster, and get them interested in what you have to say. When you have their interest, they will listen to you more closely.

Others always receive your ideas much faster and easier if you first tell them a story or example of how they can be true. If you skip the stories or examples, and tell them only the information behind the ideas you are sharing, they might be suspicious as to whether or not they are actually true. However, by telling stories or examples, others see how your ideas could be true and accept much more easily the information and the ideas you then share with them.

People buy emotionally and justify what they want to buy intellectually. It is the same when they are listening to others. People will listen to others more closely if they are emotionally engaged in what is being said rather than just intellectually engaged. Stories and examples give you the ability to reach people more on an emotional level. Once you have reached them emotionally, they are then listening to you in a much more interested way, and will listen more closely to the information you provide.

Stories and examples give you the ability to reach people more on an emotional level.

Stories and examples are important for leaders as well. Just as speakers, leaders need to communicate new ideas and information to their people, and get them motivated to take action on these new ideas and information. The best leaders do the same as the best speakers. They are constantly using stories and examples in their communications with their people.

In fact, the best leaders are often using stories and examples in the place of answers. Instead of just providing their people with the answers to their questions or problems, the best leaders tell them a story or example that helps them answer their own question or solve their own problem.

So, you can see that stories and examples are the best way for others to learn. Others learn more from applying what they learn from the stories and examples than they do from just the basic information they hear.

You can see the power in using stories and examples. When sharing any new information with others, always begin by telling a story or an example that either uses the information in it or shows how this information could be true, as the story or example provides the proof.

To become a better communicator and influencer of others, become a better storyteller. When you spark people's interest in the story or the example, you have them listening more closely to what you have to say. When they are listening closely to you, you then have the ability to influence them.

> To become a better communicator and influencer of others, become a better storyteller.

Attach any new concepts or ideas to stories and examples of how they could be true.

1. Stories and examples make the emotional link with others.
2. With stories and examples, people can see how your ideas can be true.
3. Stories and examples always keep the listener's attention.

31

Match communication
styles for a quicker
response

Communication capabilities and methods have increased over the years and today there are so many ways to communicate (email, telephone, SMS, etc.— and as always in person), but not everyone has the same preference when it comes to the way they like to communicate. How you match others' preferences can make a big difference in the effectiveness of your communications.

Think about it. You have your own preference on the way you like both to send and to receive any communications from others. You will naturally use your preferred way more than others, and if people were to take notice of how you communicate, they would use that as well.

You are more productive when others use your preferred way of communicating. If you prefer email, you will be more productive if others use email when communicating with you. However, if you were the opposite and hated email, would you really want others to email you? Probably not. Everyone has his or her preferred way of communicating.

> You are more productive when others use your preferred way of communicating.

However, getting things done, is not always only about others communicating with you, but also you communicating with others. In this case, it is more effective for you to match the preferred way of others when communicating with them.

You have probably experienced this yourself. You often try to call another person on the phone and never seem to be able to reach him or her. However, if you send an email, the same person is back to you from their BlackBerry in five minutes. Clearly, the preferred way of communicating for this person is email.

Alternatively, you also know people who really hate email. Every time you send an email, you never get a response. However, when you call him or her, you always seem to reach them right away. Again, the preferred way for this person is probably not email but phone.

It is important to keep in mind that communication is just an activity, with the real outcome of the communication being others doing what you would like them to do. By using others' preferred way of communicating, you are probably getting them to act on your communication much faster than if you used a way of communicating they didn't necessarily like. Matching others' preferred ways of communicating will get them to take action on what you want faster.

Matching others' preferred ways of communicating will get them to take action on what you want faster.

Also, if others use your preferred way of communicating, you will be far more productive. For others who regularly need to communicate with you, tell them your preferred way of communicating. The more they use your preferred way, the more productive you are.

Focus on matching others' ways of communicating and you will often get faster responses to your communications. And isn't this what communicating is all about: others responding and acting on your communications?

Tell others your preferred communication method to be more productive; and to get better action from others, use their preferred method.

1. Others using your preferred way of communicating makes you more productive.

2. Using others' preferred way of communicating always gets a faster response.

3. Matching ways of communicating can really save you time.

TRUTH

32

Listening enables better communication than talking

If you want to build relationships faster, you do it by learning more about others than others learn about you. The old saying captures this best: "How do I know how much I care about you, until I know how much you care about me?" Listening is what enables you to learn more about others, and enables better communication than talking.

Listening shows that you are interested in what others have to say. When you show interest, other people will feel more important, and making other people feel important is the fastest way to build relationships, and for others to be willing to help you in the future.

Most people's favourite topic is themselves, and this is why everyone likes to talk about him or herself. However, doing all the talking is only proving to others that you feel that you are more important than they are. Why not be different and strive to do more listening than talking?

There are many instances where people don't really like to listen in the conversations they have. What they are really doing, throughout the conversation, is thinking of what they want to say next when the opportunity comes for them to talk. You cannot give others your full attention, and truly listen to them, if you are thinking of what you want to say next all the time.

Listening becomes very powerful for you when you listen attentively, and then ask follow-up questions that will get others to share even more about what they were talking about. Successful sales people use the power of the follow-up question all the time. The more the sales person understands the customer's business and specific needs, the better he or she can deliver services to meet those needs. The same goes for you as well. The more you listen to others and ask follow-up questions, the more you will be able to influence them.

> The more you listen to others and ask follow-up questions, the more you will be able to influence them.

The first benefit of listening is one of control. When you are asking the questions and listening, you are in control of the conversations with others. If you are in control of the conversation, you are more likely to reach the result of the conversation you would like.

The second benefit of listening is what you will learn. You cannot learn more from your conversations if you are doing all the talking. When you are asking questions and listening, you get to learn more from others and this helps you to grow faster. No one can grow fast enough on just their own experiences, and by listening to others, you are able to use what you learned from their experiences and apply them to your own life.

The third benefit of listening is in the power of building relationships. You always create a better rapport, and understand better how to approach others, when you do more listening than talking. Also, nothing builds stronger relationships than making a note of the important things others say, and then remembering them sometime into the future when seeing them again. The proof of listening is in the remembering, and it is the remembering that makes others feel important. When you make others feel important, you build stronger relationships.

> The proof of listening is in the remembering, and it is the remembering that makes others feel important.

To get more done in your life, you need to surround yourself with people who are willing to help you get what you want, and to help you to help others to get what they want. Listening is the fuel that builds those key relationships.

Listening helps you to build stronger relationships with others.

1. Listen to understand, not in order to speak next.

2. Your remembering is the proof to others of your listening.

3. Listening is the fuel for building relationships with others.

TRUTH

33

No one creates success by themselves

Whatever you want to accomplish in your life, you will never be able to achieve it all on your own. No one really creates success by themselves, and in many ways, the level of success you will achieve is very much linked to how well you can work with others and get their help.

You can never accomplish everything you would like to on your own, so you will need to be able to work with others in order to achieve the success you desire. How effectively you get along with others can be a major factor in achieving that success, and your people skills are what will help you, more than any other skill, to get the right help from others.

> You can never accomplish everything you would like to on your own.

Everyone is different, and your ability to adapt to these differences will help you to get more help and achieve more in return. Far too often projects fail because two people with different personalities just couldn't get along together. Focus your energy on what you want to achieve and not on what you would have wanted to do differently from that which others are suggesting or doing.

Far too often there are people with all the abilities to achieve the success they desire, but they find it difficult to work with others and get their help to achieve it. These types of people are always struggling to work with others who don't always do things in the same way as they would. They feel uncomfortable working with others who take a different approach to the tasks to be done, and are constantly trying to get others to do it their way. However, everyone is different and they will never find others doing it exactly their way.

The people who are successful working with others and getting the help of others focus on something completely different. They are not so concerned with how it gets done, but that everyone is focused on the outcome that needs to be achieved. The successful people focus others on the outcomes that need to be achieved, and let others determine their own way to get the task done in order to achieve the outcomes.

You could say that successful people look for others who can help them achieve the *what* (the outcome), and leave it to others to determine their own *how* (the tasks) to achieve it. Successful people know how to adapt to others instead of forcing others to adapt to them. The important way is not necessarily their way, but the successful way.

You could say that your ultimate success comes through adapting yourself and serving others. Author and speaker Zig Ziglar says, "You can get everything you want in life by just helping others get what they want." Life works when you give of yourself, and always that gift gets a return for you in the form of help from others. By helping others, they will help you in return.

> By helping others, they will help you in return.

If you are a leader, by helping your people grow, they help you deliver the team's or organisation's performance, and this helps you achieve your targets as well. All successful leaders understand this and focus their energy on growing their people. By growing their people, they grow their organisation. If the organisation grows, it can deliver better performance, and then everything is reflected back on the performance of the leader who inspired the growth and performance of the organisation.

One of the traits of successful people is their willingness to teach others. By helping others to learn and grow, they will in return get the help from others as well.

Remember, no one achieves success by themselves, and the help you get from others is always a result of how you adapt to and help others first.

Success is often based on how well you interact with others.

1. Understand that you cannot create success on your own.
2. Your ability to adapt to others determines the help you will get from others.
3. The more you help others to grow, the more help they give you in return.

34

You attract help from others by keeping your commitments

You might have heard the saying, "God helps those who help themselves." You could paraphrase that by saying, "You get help from others when you keep your commitments first." Why? Because when you keep your commitments, others see helping you as a good investment of their time. When you get help from others, you are able to get more accomplished, and you often improve yourself by learning new things.

You see, how you act tells others how to interact with you. If you do not do what you said you would do, then others will prefer not to work with you. Nobody achieves success on his or her own, and you will always need the help of others. Why not be the best you can by honouring your commitments, and in this way you will attract help from others?

Many people do not realise the power that comes from keeping their commitments. In fact, most people go through life not really understanding that they have the power within themselves to influence how people will interact with them. Those who really understand this know that influence and the ability to get help from others starts by always keeping their commitments.

> Many people do not realise the power that comes from keeping their commitments.

Here's an example:

You have a problem at work and need help from someone else to solve it. There are two people in the office who could help you. One is focused in their work and always keeps his or her commitments. The other struggles to keep focused at work and often doesn't deliver on his or her commitments. Which person would you ask for help? Most likely you would ask for help from the person who keeps their commitments.

This actually works in reverse as well. Just as you would go to the people who keep their commitments for help, they would in turn be the first to help you, if you keep your commitments too. People who keep their commitments attract others who need help, but in return, they attract others to help them as well.

It all comes back to the universal principle of "the more you give, the more you get". However, it is also, in this case, "the more you have commitment, the more commitment you get from others", and also the help to achieve what you want to achieve in your life.

People will always take the time to help others who they know have the commitment within them. It really is strange that the very people who need the help the most don't often get it. Just as you read in the example, people really don't want either to ask for help or to help people who don't keep their commitments. Why? Because people who don't keep commitments cannot be trusted as much as others, and this is why these people are generally avoided.

> People will always take the time to help others who they know have the commitment within them.

You have realised the importance of keeping your commitments. When you focus yourself on keeping your commitments, you will probably end up making fewer commitments than before. If you are like others, you have been making commitments that were more "I'll try" than "It will definitely happen".

When you focus on keeping your commitments, you also get another benefit in return. You get the increase in your own self-esteem and respect for yourself, as you have not only kept your commitments with others, but you are also keeping your commitments with yourself.

When you begin to keep the commitments with yourself, it then becomes much easier to keep the commitments with others. Start from today, and focus on keeping your commitments and attracting help from others in getting things done.

The way you act is either attracting people to help you or sending them away.

1. If you keep your commitments, others will keep their commitments to you.

2. People will always help others who help themselves first.

3. Keeping commitments to yourself helps you keep commitments to others.

35

Trust is the fuel for productive teamwork

Nobody creates success on his or her own. To get things done, you will always be a part of a team, and trust is the fuel that creates productive teamwork. Teamwork is really getting everyone to work together to achieve a common outcome, and people who trust each other will work more productively with each other to achieve it.

You build trust by getting to know others and learning more about both their professional and personal lives. It is often what you learn about other people's personal lives that provides you with more insight into how they think and feel, as well as what is most important to them. When you know people better, you will understand better their behaviours, and then know how best to interact with them to create better teamwork.

The key to building trust is to be comfortable enough to share your opinions with others, even when your opinions will differ from theirs. You know that you have high trust in your team when everyone is willing to open up and share his or her ideas and opinions.

To build trust and maintain it, you always need to allow for the differences in others. The very best teams do not have members who are all the same types of person. The differences in the team can be a real strength, and can help the team to develop more creative solutions. However, to make it work and to get the benefits, everyone needs to adapt a little to allow for the differences of others. Your ability to adapt your approaches to others can be one of the most important abilities for you in getting things done through others. In fact, one of the key skills of successful leaders is their ability to adapt.

> To build trust and maintain it, you always need to allow for the differences in others.

Conflict is something that many people want to avoid, especially in a team environment. However, conflict, if constructive around the issues, is something that makes for much stronger teams. Teams with high trust experience much greater conflict than teams with little trust. Teams with little trust often don't have any conflict, as everyone is afraid to bring up anything that others might disagree with. If your team has little or no conflict, you don't really have a high performing team, as people are not willing to share what they really are thinking.

You will often need to work in teams in order to get things done, and they will help you achieve what you want to achieve. To make this happen, you always need to be a "participating" team member and help the team drive towards the outcomes that will create success for both you and the team. You see so many people who don't really "participate" in the teams they belong to. These people usually attend all the meetings but never really speak at all. They are not offering their ideas, and never really contribute to the team, apart from their required work outside the meetings.

Set yourself the goal always to be a participating team member. When you participate, you are "voicing your say" on both the direction and the focus of the team. By "participating", you have a greater opportunity to make sure that you can achieve success for both you and the team.

> Set yourself the goal always to be a participating team member.

To build trust and get the help of others, create an environment where everyone will participate and share what is really on their mind. With this type of environment, your team meetings will never be boring, and you will put "everything" on the table to be discussed, openly in the meeting rather than in much more personal ways in the hallways.

Set your goal to *build trust* in whatever teams you are a part of. Trust drives teamwork.

Focus on developing trust with your fellow team members.

1. Trust enables people to share what they are thinking.
2. The best solutions and outcomes are a result of every team member participating.
3. If your team meetings are boring, then you have low trust in your team.

36

You get the behaviours that you reinforce

Let's say you have to complete four different tasks for four different people by tomorrow. Three never follow up with you, but the fourth calls you in the morning and asks if you will complete it by tomorrow and if you need any help. Which task would you do first? That of the person who follows up, as their follow-up gets you doing their task first.

There will always be situations where you need something from others by a certain date in order to keep your commitment to another. How you reinforce (follow up) the *right* behaviours of others to keep their commitment not only helps them deliver on time in this situation, but in all future situations as well.

Take a situation where you need some work from another person by Wednesday in order for you to meet your commitment of delivering work by Friday. If you politely follow up with the other person on Tuesday, and ask if they can complete their work by the next day, then you have much more confidence that their work will be done on time. Also, you have set the image in the other person's mind that this is important, and they will then probably give it higher priority in their mind as well. You have reinforced the right behaviours because you followed up.

Take this same situation with a slightly different example. You have the same commitments, their work needs to be done by Wednesday, and your work and commitment to others is by Friday. However, this time you do not follow up until Friday morning, the day your commitment is due. By following up so late, you are now putting pressure on the other person to deliver quickly so that you can keep your commitment. Do you think they will appreciate that extra pressure? Do you appreciate the extra pressure you have just put on yourself by not following up sooner? Probably not.

There's also another aspect in this second example. Because you didn't follow up until two days after the day you told the other person you needed their work by, they now think that your actual requested dates are not the true requested dates. The next time you need work from them and request a date, they will think that they actually have a couple of extra days to complete it, and will probably not put the same priority on meeting your requested date.

You can see that the way you follow up, or the lack of follow-up, has an impact on the behaviours of others. The examples show that you get the behaviours you reinforce.

These situations and examples are about just following up. However, the way you reinforce others' behaviours can make a difference in many other situations.

The way you follow up, or the lack of follow-up, has an impact on the behaviours of others.

For leaders and even parents, how they reinforce the behaviours in their employees and in their children, respectively, is really establishing their behaviours, both today and into the future. For you, just as leaders and parents, how you reinforce the behaviours of others establishes how they will interact with you, both today and into the future.

The best approach is to establish boundaries up front as to what you will consider both good and bad behaviour. When it is discussed up front, there are far less misunderstandings. Then, it is all about how you reinforce those behaviours:

1. For good behaviours, thank others for what they did. Give them praise.

2. For bad behaviours (outside the boundaries), remind them of what they did and why it is a problem, both for you and for them.

You can see that what you can do to help others deliver on their commitments to you is the same as what leaders and parents need to do as well.

You get the behaviours you reinforce (either with your actions or with your inaction).

1. Reinforce both the good and bad behaviour of others.

2. Always follow up, especially when your credibility is on the line.

3. Follow-up says that the task is important, and not following up means the opposite.

37

You can't see the picture when you are in the frame

In order to become better at getting things done, you have to get better yourself. You cannot always see what those improvements need to be, and it is often the feedback that you receive from others that enables you to focus on the *right* things to improve. It really is true. You can't see the picture when you are in the frame.

You always need feedback from others to help you see those areas in your life where you could really improve. In business, you often have 360 degree feedback, where you get feedback from people above you, your peers and people below you. This feedback gives you some idea of the areas in your life where your behaviours could be improved.

Everyone has blind spots in their behaviours that they do not see themselves. If you go through life not getting any feedback from others, then these blind spots stay invisible to you forever, and you have no way to improve them. You cannot improve an area or behaviours in your life that you are not aware of.

Everyone has blind spots in their behaviours that they do not see themselves.

In order to understand these blind spots, you cannot just count on others always to point them out to you. Your family and friends, who are close to you, are often hesitant to talk to you about any of your bad areas or bad behaviours.

Getting yourself to see the picture is all about your taking the initiative to ask for feedback, and not waiting for others to come forward with it. If others come forward with feedback on their own, it is often not in a constructive way, but more in a negative way. When they come with this type of feedback, then you are probably not in the right "mood" to listen to it anyway.

The best approach to see the picture is to ask one of your close friends or co-workers to help you with the areas or behaviours they think you could improve on. Ask them for both your strengths and your weaknesses, and from their perspective, what area or behaviours you should focus on for improvement. This advice could be very valuable in helping you to improve, grow and become the person who can achieve the goals you have defined and to accomplish what you want with your life.

It is important to ask about both your strengths and your weaknesses. Your strengths are what make you successful today. So, you should always be focusing on improving those weaknesses that will help you use your strengths even better. The more you are able to use your strengths, the more success you will be able to achieve. As a priority always focus first on those weaknesses that prevent you from using your strengths to the fullest.

> The more you are able to use your strengths, the more success you will be able to achieve.

So, if feedback from others will help you improve yourself faster and grow faster, why don't you ask for feedback regularly from others? It is human nature not to want to hear negative things about yourself from others. You would not really have the motivation to ask for this feedback.

However, you do see others who are constantly asking for feedback, and these are the very people who are also very successful. What is the trait that drives them to ask for this feedback and for others not to ask? Often, it comes down to the confidence that successful people have in themselves. They know that they will improve themselves faster by getting feedback from others, and that without feedback, they will never be able to take the action and improve on those "blind spots" in their behaviours. They understand that the more they improve, the more successful they can become.

It makes sense, doesn't it? So, the place to start is to build your confidence strong enough that it enables you to ask for feedback from others. The people who get ahead in life and achieve success are constantly asking for feedback. They know that their success will only continue as long as they are growing, and that feedback will help them keep growing, and growing faster than without it.

Honest feedback always makes you better. Why not ask for feedback from others today?

1. Ask trusted friends or co-workers for feedback.

2. Understand both your strengths and your weaknesses.

3. Focus your improvements on those weaknesses that stop you from using your strengths better.

TRUTH

38

Growth comes when you are comfortable being uncomfortable

Think back to all the occasions when you were doing something new for the first time. Were you feeling comfortable when you were first trying it? Probably not, if you are like everyone else. If you try new things you will be learning and growing, and also feeling a little uncomfortable.

Growth really comes when you are trying to do something new or you are experiencing new situations. However, you often try to avoid these new things because of the fear that you might not do them right the first time or behave in the right way.

People very rarely do anything perfectly the first time they try it. It makes perfect sense, but this is often forgotten when people avoid doing something because they think they might not do it right and might make a mistake. Think about this. If you are totally comfortable with what you are doing now, are you really challenging yourself and are you growing?

> People very rarely do anything perfectly the first time they try it.

The successful people who get ahead in life are constantly challenging themselves to try new things, and to attempt to do something they have never done before. They know that growth comes when they are moving forward and stretching themselves to use the abilities and the potential that they see inside them. Also, they know that they will make mistakes along the way, and that this is simply part of the learning process of trying something new, and especially in trying something new for the first time.

You could say that successful people have a goal always to be a little "uncomfortable". They believe that if they are totally comfortable with what they are doing, they are then not growing, and that not growing will limit their future success. If you are always comfortable, are you growing?

Take the example of people who are afraid to speak in public. It is often said that this is one of the biggest fears in people's lives, to speak in public. What people are afraid of is being uncomfortable and possibly making a mistake. However, you could ask any successful speaker, and they could probably tell you that there were many times when they made mistakes in their speeches, but that did not stop them from being successful. In fact, it has been because of their drive to try new things and be uncomfortable at first (and make a few mistakes) that they have grown faster and become more successful. They didn't let being uncomfortable stop them from growing.

How about you? Are you totally comfortable in everything that you are doing today? Are you letting being uncomfortable stop you from growing?

Why not set a goal for yourself that you will always try something new in at least one part of your life each and every week? If you are trying something new in every part of your life all at once, this can be a little stressful and overwhelming. However, most people are trying almost nothing new and seem to live a life of "routine".

Take a look at your life today. Are there areas of your life where you are totally comfortable and have locked yourself into a routine? Take a good look at those areas and see what "uncomfortable" growth opportunities you have been avoiding, and focus yourself to take action on those opportunities this very week. Remember, being a little uncomfortable equals *growing*.

> Remember, being a little uncomfortable equals *growing*.

Set the goal for yourself to get comfortable being a little uncomfortable, and you will always be growing and moving closer to the goals you have defined and what you want to accomplish in your life.

Success comes faster when you are comfortable being a little uncomfortable.

1. Never be afraid to try something new and grow.
2. Understand that no one really does anything perfectly the first time they try it.
3. Become comfortable being a little uncomfortable.

39

Comparing yourself to others limits your growth

You often compare yourself to others. Some comparisons make you feel good, as you are thinking you are doing better than they are. Other comparisons make you feel bad, or at least make you feel that you could do more. However, all comparisons with others have a limit to their impact on you. The only comparison with no limit is comparing yourself to your potential.

The only comparison with no limit is comparing yourself to your potential.

Let's take a look at the golfer Tiger Woods. He and other people at the top of their sports are almost always comparing themselves to their potential, rather than to others. In the case of Tiger Woods, if he compared himself to others, he could then tend to relax a bit and slow down the development of his own golf game. In fact, Tiger is one of the golfers who practises and works on his golf game the most, and he recently commented that there is a great deal of improvement he can make in his own golf game. Tiger's focus is not on comparing himself to others, but on comparing himself to the potential that he sees inside him.

How about you? Do you compare yourself to others or to your potential? Everyone has different abilities, and success in life and getting things done is always about using those abilities to the fullest. Legendary American football coach Vince Lombardi said, "The measure of who we are is what we do with what we have." If you are like others, you have more within you than what you are using today.

There are many people who are using their abilities just to get by. They have such a great potential within them, but instead of investing the time to develop that potential, they go on year after year just using it to live the life of just getting by. How about you? Are you developing the potential that is within you or just using it to get by?

Scientists say that everyone is using only a fraction of the abilities they have. With that being so, you, like everyone else, have the potential in you to accomplish a great deal more than what you are currently accomplishing today.

The focus should never be on comparing yourself to others, but on comparing yourself to your potential. In fact, most people have never even given any thought to what that potential is that is inside them. Have you? Why not invest the time to think through the potential that is inside you and how you can take action on leveraging it to get what you want (that success you have defined)? The more you think about your potential, the more action you will take each and every day to use that potential.

> The more you think about your potential, the more action you will take each and every day to use that potential.

By focusing on your potential and not on others, your only limiting factor in leveraging that potential to get what you want is just the belief in yourself that you can do it (and that's all within your control).

Remember, learn from others and their experiences, but never compare yourself to others. Focus your thoughts and energy on your potential. By focusing on your potential, you will grow to become the person who can achieve your goals and accomplish what you want in your life.

1. Compare yourself to your potential and not to others.
2. Everyone has within themselves the potential for success.
3. Only those who remind themselves of their potential will ever really use it.

TRUTH

40

Surround yourself with the *right* people to fuel your growth

You don't achieve success all by yourself. Also, you cannot really learn enough or grow fast enough if you only rely on your own experiences to bring you this growth. You can read books and do your own personal development to help you grow, but you also need to meet and interact with people who will challenge your thinking and help you grow even faster.

Publisher, motivator and humorist Charlie "Tremendous" Jones said, "You will be the same five years from now except for two things: the books you read and the people you meet." You grow through your self-study, as well as through the people you meet and can learn from. In order to grow faster, you need to surround yourself with the right people who can help you grow. Are the people you surround yourself with today helping you grow?

Think about the people you meet on a daily and weekly basis in both your professional and personal lives. Are these people helping you grow to become the person you would like to be? Are they helping you achieve the success you would like to achieve? And, lastly, are they helping you find enjoyment and fulfilment on the journey towards that success you desire?

These are great questions to ask yourself. If you are like others, your success might be slowed down by the people you surround yourself with the most. That sounds a little negative, but if you think about it, you can see how that may be true.

You surround yourself with people who make you feel comfortable, and that's especially true for your personal life. You want to feel relaxed around the people you are with. However, you grow most when you are uncomfortable. If this is true, keeping the same people around you all the time is probably slowing your growth. If your growth is being slowed, then you can imagine that the pace to reach your goals and what you want is being slowed as well.

Keeping the same people around you all the time is probably slowing your growth.

You can see the impact of surrounding yourself with the right people on the lives of today's successful people.

Everyone knows the UK's Simon Cowell, the judge who "tells it like it is" on the UK X Factor show and the US American Idol show. If you were to ask Simon about the people who helped make him a success, he would probably mention the name Pete Waterman. Early in Simon's career, he followed Pete Waterman around and learned a great deal about the music business from him, with this becoming what he would probably describe as "the foundation for his success".

Let's take another example. Look at Tony Robbins, the American motivational speaker, and someone who has made an impact on millions of lives. When Tony was younger, he worked for another great speaker—Jim Rohn. Again, if you asked Tony about the people who helped shape his thinking and helped him succeed, he would mention Jim Rohn's name.

Both Simon Cowell and Tony Robbins chose to be around people whom they could learn from and who could help them grow. Who could you invest more time in getting closer to and be around, in order for you to grow faster as well?

There's an old saying that "your network creates your net worth". Whom you know and spend the most time with is one of the most powerful indicators of your future success and net worth. Given the success you have defined for yourself and the goals that will help drive you to reach it, don't you think one of the most important actions for you to take is to define who can help you grow and reach your goals faster?

> Whom you know and spend the most time with is one of the most powerful indicators of your future success and net worth.

Invest a few minutes this very day and think about what types of people and who specifically could help you the most. When you have this list, then think about what are the possible ways to put yourself in a better position to meet these people and to get to know them better. This could be through formal networks and through utilising the people you already know.

The truth is, if you haven't really defined who can help you the most, you will never take the necessary actions to put yourself in a position to meet them.

Surround yourself with people who will help you grow.

1. Take a look at the people you spend your most time with.

2. Are they helping you grow as fast as you would like to?

3. Your network creates your net worth.

TRUTH

41

Pride in what you do creates excellence in what you do

Think back in your life, and you will find a time when you did an exceptional job on a particular assignment, whether it was during your school days or in your work. If you think about it, you will most likely find that you took great pride in what you accomplished, and that pride was most likely the reason you did it so well in the first place.

For you to get things done, the same drive for quality and pride in your work can drive you to accomplish great things. Pride always gets driven by the commitment you have behind what you are doing, as commitment drives ownership.

> Pride always gets driven by the commitment you have behind what you are doing, as commitment drives ownership.

You see the difference pride makes when you consider how you treat your own car compared with a rental car. Whenever you rent a car, you often don't take care of the car as you would your own. You probably don't wash it when it is dirty, as you will probably only make use of it for a very short time. You just don't have the pride of ownership to take care of the car as if it were your own.

However, could you imagine a time when you might take pride in that rental car and treat it more as if it were your own? What if you had rented this car for business and were using it to visit customers? If the car was very dirty, would that have given a good impression to the customers you were visiting? In this particular case, you would probably wash the car before visiting your customers, as you have now taken some pride in being able to make a good impression on your customers.

Pride in what you do is more about how you go about your day-to-day activities than about any big initiatives or changes you could make. It is about always looking to do your best on what you could call "the fundamentals". These are usually all the common activities you do during your day. However, the people who take pride in their work always do these common activities to the best of their abilities.

How you do these common activities, day in and day out, is what will always provide the foundation of your success. The foundation of success is doing the necessary, when it is necessary, and always doing it to the best of your abilities.

In today's world, there are far too many people who are constantly acting as if just acceptable is good enough. When you don't have the pride in your work, you always seem to do only the minimum and often just produce acceptable quality that's good enough. However, if you keep repeating this way of working, the quality associated with good enough always seems to get lower and lower. Whenever you settle for good enough, you will tend to settle for less in the future as well. It is as if you are constantly lowering your standards as long as no one else is complaining. However, at the same time you are constantly lowering the pride you have in your own work as well.

> **Whenever you settle for good enough, you will tend to settle for less in the future as well.**

People who have pride in their work will always strive to produce their very best, and it is only by focusing on doing your best that you keep your pride strong as well. How about you? Are you always striving to do your best in all situations and circumstances?

Remember, pride in doing the necessary when it is necessary will help you get things done, today and every day and always to the best of your abilities.

1. Doing your best will always create pride in your work.
2. When you have pride in your work, you always accomplish more.
3. Building commitment creates ownership, and ownership creates pride.

TRUTH

42

It is all about making common sense common practice

In all the truths you have read, you probably didn't see any earth shattering concepts, tools or techniques that will help you improve how you get things done. That's very interesting, isn't it? However, what you have read are many common sense ideas that all successful people have used to get things done and achieve success over the years, and as far back as history shows.

What you get done and accomplish in your life does not depend on coming up with fantastic ideas every day and doing something different. It comes down to taking the necessary common sense actions and having the discipline to actually keep doing them, day in and day out.

Many people will lack the discipline to implement the habits that make common sense common practice. These actions are always easy to do, and there's nothing that requires you to have a PhD degree to do them. However, because these actions are so easy to do, they are also easy not to do.

> **Many people will lack the discipline to implement the habits that make common sense common practice.**

You have read many truths that talk about how to get things done by yourself and along with others, and these have covered many areas. However, you could really summarise what you have learned in just a couple of common sense actions:

1. Defining what you want? *Success.*
2. Deciding what you need to do on a daily and weekly basis to get it? *Discipline.*

Common sense says that you cannot hit a target you do not have.

So, if you want to be great at getting the *right* things done, you have to start by defining very clearly what you want and why you want it.

Also, common sense says that you cannot get different results by doing the same things.

You probably already know what you really should be doing on a daily and weekly basis to get what you want. If you are like others, *the problem is never in the knowing, only in the doing.*

Take some of the ideas from the other truths and make the decision to put those daily and weekly habits in your life from this very day. No one can do this for you, and no one knows what you want and why you want it more than you. Jim Rohn says it best: "You can't hire someone else to do your push ups for you." In fact, it is simply a decision you need to make, and then you must make a commitment to yourself to take the necessary actions that are behind that decision.

> No one knows what you want and why you want it more than you.

What common sense do you need to make common practice today?

Pick one common sense habit that would move you closer to the success you want and the life you want to live. Create a plan of action that will ensure you make the habit a real habit. If what you want is so important to you and the *why* so big that you have to have it, then it will be much easier for you to keep that commitment to yourself and create that habit.

In *The Truth About Getting Things Done*, you have realised that it is almost always about you, your focus and the discipline behind that focus rather than about any particular tool or time management technique. Also, you want to get things done for a purpose, achieving something you want, not just ticking off completed tasks.

Here's a word to remember and three key points that utilise the letters in the word. It summarises a great approach to get you started.

The word is **WHY**!

1. **W**hat **success** do you **W**ant and **W**hy do you want it?
2. **H**ow can you **get it done** (the outcomes and your **H**abits) and what **H**elp do you need from others?
3. Who do **Y**ou need to become and what discipline do **Y**ou need to put into creating the daily and weekly habits that will enable you to get it done and **achieve** the success you desire?

Make common sense common practice—which is the uncommon thing to do!

(Key Word)—Highlights the subject related to each reference.

Truth 1

Les Brown, *Step into your Greatness Live*, www.tstn.com (Potential)

Brian Tracy, *Brian Tracy Success Mastery Academy*, Strategic Marketing Group, 1998 (Clarity)

Nido Qubein, http://www.nidoqubein.com (Future)

Truth 2

George Zalucki, *An Experience to Make a Difference*, www.georgezalucki.com, 1992 (Why, desire)

Truth 3

Les Brown, *Step into your Greatness Live*, www.tstn.com (Belief)

Denis Waitley, *Winners Believe with Passion*, www.tstn.com (Belief)

Truth 4

Brian Tracy, *Brian Tracy Success Mastery Academy*, Strategic Marketing Group, 1998 (Focus)

Stan Christensen, Stanford University—Entrepreneurial Thought Leader Podcasts, http://edcorner.stanford.edu/authorMaterialInfo.html?author=211 (Criteria)

Truth 5

Brian Tracy, *Brian Tracy Success Mastery Academy*, Strategic Marketing Group, 1998 (Focus)

Truth 6

Brian Tracy, *Brian Tracy Success Mastery Academy*, Strategic Marketing Group, 1998 (Clarity)

Truth 7

Brian Tracy, *Brian Tracy Success Mastery Academy*, Strategic Marketing Group, 1998 (Goals)

Truth 8

Jim Rohn, *The Art of Exceptional Living*, Nightingale-Conant, 2003 (Journey)

Earl Nightingale, http://earlnightingale.com (Belief)

Denis Waitley, *Winners Determine Their Futures*, www.tstn.com (Future)

Truth 9

David Allen, *Getting Things Done: The Art of Stress-Free Productivity*, Penguin, 2002 (Follow-up)

Bill Creech, *The Five Pillars of TQM* (Ownership)

Truth 10

Dr Maxwell Maltz, http://www.psycho-cybernetics.com/maltz.html (Thought)

Robert H. Schuller, http://www.crystalcathedral.org (Thought)

Les Brown, *Step into your Greatness Live*, www.tstn.com (Belief)

George Zalucki, *Emotions—Servants or Destroyers*, www.georgezalucki.com, 1992 (Belief)

Bob Proctor, *Getting to Know You*, www.tstn.com (Paradigms)

Truth 11

Jim Rohn, *The Art of Exceptional Living*, Nightingale-Conant, 2003 (Today)

John Wooden, *Wooden*, McGraw-Hill, 1997 (Today)

Truth 12

Dan Lier, America's Coach, *Your True Potential*, www.tstn.com (Belief)

Les Brown, *Step into your Greatness Live,* www.tstn.com (Belief)

Truth 13

Zig Ziglar, *See You at the Top*, Pelican Publishing Company, 2nd revised edition, 2000 (Attitude)

Rick Pitino, *Lead to Succeed, 10 Traits of Great Leadership in Business and Life*, Broadway, 2001 (Choice)

Truth 14

James Allen, http://www.asamanthinketh.net/JamesAllen.htm (Thoughts)

Brian Tracy, *Brian Tracy Success Mastery Academy*, Strategic Marketing Group, 1998 (Thoughts)

David Allen, *Getting Things Done: The Art of Stress-Free Productivity*, Penguin, 2002 (Next action)

Truth 15

Jerry Clark, *Think Like a Giant*, www.tstn.com and www.clubrhino.com (Thoughts)

Truth 16

Jim Rohn, *The Art of Exceptional Living*, Nightingale-Conant, 2003 (Action)

Truth 17

David Allen, *Getting Things Done: The Art of Stress-Free Productivity*, Penguin, 2002 (Think ahead, rapid refocusing)

Truth 18

David Allen, *Getting Things Done: The Art of Stress-Free Productivity*, Penguin, 2002 (Think ahead)

Rick Pitino, *Lead to Succeed, 10 Traits of Great Leadership in Business and Life*, Broadway, 2001 (Prepare)

Truth 19

Les Brown, *Step into your Greatness Live*, www.tstn.com (Action)

George Zalucki, *Emotions—Servants or Destroyers*, www.georgezalucki.com, 1992 (Action)

Truth 20

John Wooden, *Wooden*, McGraw-Hill, 1997 (Today)

Truth 21

Jim Rohn, *The Art of Exceptional Living*, Nightingale-Conant, 2003 (Discipline)

Jim Cathcart, *The Purpose of Selling*, www.tstn.com (Discipline)

Truth 22

Brad Isaac, http://www.fromedwardwithlove.com/jerry-seinfelds-productivity-secret (Daily discipline)

Truth 23

Brian Tracy, *Brian Tracy Success Mastery Academy*, Strategic Marketing Group, 1998 (Extra)

Truth 24

Jim Rohn, *The Art of Exceptional Living*, Nightingale-Conant, 2003 (Action)

Robert H. Schuller, http://www.crystalcathedral.org (Action)

Truth 25

Denis Waitley, Platinum Collection, *The Psychology of Winning*, Nightingale-Conant, Abridged edition, 2005 (Habits)

Truth 26

Tony Alessandra, *The Platinum Rule*, www.tstn.com (Adaptability)

Truth 27

George Zalucki, *Emotions—Servants or Destroyers*, www.georgezalucki.com, 1992 (Listen)

Truth 28

Jeffrey Gitomer, *Little Red Book of Selling*, Bard Press, 1st edition, 2004 (Sales)

Zig Ziglar, *See You at the Top*, Pelican Publishing Company, 2nd revised edition, 2000 (Sales)

Truth 29

Larry Bossidy, Ram Charan and Charles Burck, *Execution: The Discipline of Getting Things Done*, Crown Business, 1st edition, 2002 (Questions)

Jack Welch and John A. Byrne, *Jack: Straight from the Gut*, Business Plus, 2003 (Questions)

Truth 30

Jim Rohn, *The Art of Exceptional Living*, Nightingale-Conant, 2003 (Stories)

Truth 31

David Allen, *Getting Things Done: The Art of Stress-Free Productivity*, Penguin, 2002 (Communication)

Truth 32

Jeffrey Gitomer, *Little Red Book of Selling*, Bard Press, 1st edition, 2004 (Listen)

Connie Podesta, *Life Would Be Easy If It Weren't for Other People*, Corwin Press, 1st edition, 1999 (Listen)

Truth 33

Tony Alessandra, *The Platinum Rule*, www.tstn.com (Adaptability)

Zig Ziglar, http://www.ziglar.com (Serve)

Truth 35

Patrick M. Lencioni, *The Five Dysfunctions of a Team: A Leadership Fable*, Jossey-Bass, 1st edition, 2002 (Trust, conflict)

Patrick M. Lencioni, Leadership TRAQ Podcast, http://www.leadershiptraq.com/podcast/traqpod.html (Trust)

Truth 36

David Allen, *Getting Things Done: The Art of Stress-Free Productivity*, Penguin, 2002 (Follow-up)

Patrick M. Lencioni, Leadership TRAQ Podcast, http://www.leadershiptraq.com/podcast/traqpod.html (Trust)

Larry Bossidy, Ram Charan and Charles Burck, *Execution: The Discipline of Getting Things Done*, Crown Business, 1st edition, 2002 (Follow-up)

Truth 37

Les Brown, *Step into your Greatness Live*, www.tstn.com (Potential)

Marcus Buckingham and Curt Coffman, *First Break All the Rules: What the World's Greatest Managers Do Differently*, Simon & Schuster, 1st edition, 1999 (Strengths)

Truth 38

George Zalucki, *Emotions—Servants or Destroyers*, www.georgezalucki.com, 1992 (Uncomfortable)

Steve Siebold, *Developing Mental Toughness Skills*, www.tstn.com (Thoughts)

Truth 39

Vince Lombardi, http://www.vincelombardi.com/about/highlights.htm (Potential)

Dan Lier, America's Coach, *Your True Potential*, www.tstn.com (Potential)

Truth 40

Charlie "Tremendous" Jones, http://www.executivebooks.com/cjones (Network)

Les Brown, *Step into your Greatness Live*, www.tstn.com (Potential)

Steve Young, Stanford University—Entrepreneurial Thought Leader Podcasts, http://edcorner.stanford.edu/authorMaterialInfo.html?mid=1739 (Trust)

Truth 41

Bill Creech, *The Five Pillars of TQM* (Ownership)

Truth 42

Jim Rohn, *The Art of Exceptional Living*, Nightingale-Conant, 2003 (Discipline)

About the Author

Mark Fritz is the founder of **Procedor**, a company focused on two main areas—personal effectiveness *(leading yourself)* and leadership effectiveness *(leading others)*—and provides consulting, training and coaching/mentoring services to companies throughout the world. Mark has lived in the USA, Singapore, Egypt, Netherlands, Italy, Japan and the UK, and has successfully combined best practices from around the world to create an innovative set of business tools and insights that can help businesses of all sizes be even more successful.

He is an associate of Ashridge College in the UK, co-teaching Leading Complex Teams, and a visiting professor teaching Virtual Leadership at the HEC in France, at the Instituto de Empresa in Spain and at IFL—Stockholm School of Economics in Sweden. Mark's natural charm and personable style, enhanced by a great sense of humour, has made him a speaker of choice at company events and seminars. He is an affiliate of the prestigious CSA Celebrity Speakers and regularly speaks on Personal Effectiveness for Leaders and Virtual Leadership (Leading People at a Distance).

Mark is also the author of *Time to Get Started*, a compilation of his best daily thoughts from the first 18 months of writing. You can read Mark's daily thoughts at: www.procedor.com/daily-thought.html

Visit him at: www.procedor.com

Acknowledgements

No one can accomplish anything without the inspiration and help of others, and this book is no exception. Whatever we accomplish in life is really enabled by the strong foundation of what we have learned from others. A strong foundation of information, insights and ideas brings us more inspiration, energy and creativity in **getting things done**.

The information, ideas and insights of Brian Tracy, Les Brown, David Allen, Zig Ziglar, General Bill Creech, George Zalucki, Jeffrey Gitomer, Jerry Clark, Dan Lier, Denis Waitley, Tony Alessandra, Jim Rohn, Jack Welch and John Wooden have all helped over the years to create a strong foundation from which this book was inspired.

Lastly, to my wife Atsuko for all her support and encouragement.

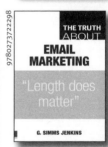